THE POWER

OF A

DREAM

Dr Leanne Destiny Armitage

The Power of A Dream

The 7 Steps to Ignite Your Dreams, Subdue Your Fears and Live an Extraordinary Life

© Copyright 2022 by Dr Leanne Armitage

ISBN number - 978-1-80068-686-1

Paperback Version

Printed in the United Kingdom

Independently Published

Table of Contents

Introduction

Thank you for not only picking up my book, but opening it!

My name is Dr Leanne Armitage and I am a medical doctor, inspirational speaker, multi-award-winning leader and co-founder of The Armitage Foundation – a charity committed to increasing diversity across UK medical schools. Despite the many hats I wear, my journey towards success was not a straightforward one. I have overcome great odds to stand as the woman I am today. Through my story I want to encourage everyone, no matter how young or old, that irrespective of your background, you can go on to achieve your dreams! You can manifest the greatness that resides inside of you.

I grew up in a single parent home on a council estate in Peckham, which at the time, was one of the most deprived areas in London. I met my biological father for the first time at 19 years old, shortly after starting medical school. This meant that growing up I did not have the guidance of a father figure. I come from a family of zero medics and out of my mother's five children, only one other went to university. Studying at university wasn't the culture in my family... My mother left high school with no qualifications and did not know how to navigate the higher education system. My older sister, Annette, who was my only sibling who studied at university, became my makeshift mentor. Despite lacking insight into the medical profession, herself, she did her best to guide me in the right direction. She was, and continues to be, a powerful force for good in my life and the catalyst behind much of my success. My sister is truly my real-life hero.

Growing up I battled with low self-esteem, partly because I struggled to identify with any relatable role models. My dream for the future seemed far greater than the environment I was growing up in, which made me question whether achieving it was even possible. In fact, I would often ask myself the question "Is it possible for me to achieve something I have never seen anyone else around me achieve?"

Despite the odds stacked against me, not only have I been able to realise my dream of becoming a doctor, I have exceeded this beyond my wildest imagination. Along my journey I have been awarded by Her Majesty the Queen, interacted with heads of government, co-founded a multi-award-winning charity, won numerous leadership awards and have had a range of amazing public speaking opportunities. I have been able to use my voice to share my story of the power of a dream. For it was my deep yearning to achieve my dream that enabled me to dodge, jump and crush various obstacles standing in my way. I hope that through reading this book, not only will you be inspired to dream, but you too, will find the inner strength to overcome any obstacles that may be standing in your way. I hope that you'll be inspired to go on your own journey of self-transformation so that you can become the very best version of yourself.

For truly, you are the captain of your ship and the master of your destiny.

Thank you once again for picking up my book! I hope my story empowers you to manifest the greatness that resides inside of   you.

Part I

The Birth and
Manifestation of My Dream

Chapter 1

The Birth of My Dream

When I was 15 years old, I made the decision that I wanted to become a trauma surgeon. A trauma surgeon is a surgeon who specialises in managing patients with traumatic injuries, such as car crash injuries or gunshot wounds. I made this decision because I witnessed the aftermath of a traumatic event.

My sister and I were returning from a shopping trip we did earlier that day. We were about three minutes away from home when we heard a roaring sound from above. Startled by the noise, I looked to the sky and saw the propellers of a red helicopter. They were cutting through the wind as the helicopter made its descent towards a grass field in the middle of a huge estate close to where we were living at the time. I have always loved helicopters and so when I saw that the helicopter was landing nearby, I was filled to the brim with excitement. I eagerly asked my sister if we could watch the helicopter land and she agreed. Together we briskly walked towards the grass field. As we drew closer my excitement grew stronger and stronger. When we arrived at the scene, I saw a crowd of people gathered around, I could count about 20 people standing there. However, I immediately noticed that something wasn't quite right. I could feel an eerie energy in the atmosphere and the facial expressions of the people standing in front of me did not mirror the excitement I felt inside. Trying to make sense of what was going on, I turned to the closest person to me and asked why the helicopter had landed. A woman with brown hair turned to me and her response drained every ounce of excitement from my body. She told me a young man had been stabbed. In that moment, I felt a deep sense of grief as it dawned on me that this helicopter hadn't landed for any good reason at all, but rather, because a young man was fighting for his life. The feeling of grief then became intertwined with a sense of anger and frustration as I looked around thinking, *everyone is just standing here staring but who is actually going to do something to make a difference? Who is going to do something to end this horrific cycle of young black men killing each other through the bullet of a gun, or the blade of a knife?* I then remember feeling a sense of disempowerment as I thought, *what can I do? I'm just a 15-year-old girl!* I asked my sister if we could go home and together, we strolled back.

When I arrived home that evening, I went straight to my bedroom. My heart felt aggrieved in a way I hadn't experienced before. Perhaps it was because my emotions transitioned so quickly from sheer excitement to grief. Growing up in Peckham, the sad reality is that it was not uncommon to hear about young men losing their lives due to knife and gun crime. It has been something that has always made me feel distressed, especially because many of these young men were teenagers who were not far from my age. I found it worrying that their lives could be so easily lost over the most seemingly trivial things and in the most horrific ways. I knew it was wrong and I always wanted to help but I wasn't quite sure how. That evening, I sat on my bedroom floor for hours. I meditated and prayed asking God, "What can I do to make a difference?" It was during this time that the idea of becoming a trauma surgeon came to me. My logic was that if I aspired to become a trauma surgeon, it would give me a platform to go into environments where young men were involved in knife and gun crime, in the hope of inspiring them to be and do better. I reasoned that working as a trauma surgeon in London would mean that I would treat the victims of knife and gun crime which would provide a gateway for me to go into the communities where they were based to speak to them.

I wasn't certain that this would be the resolution to the problem. After all, I was only 15 years old and I didn't understand the depth and breadth of the issue. However, this idea empowered me. It allowed me to channel the grief and frustration I was feeling into something positive. It gave me a deep sense of meaning and a mission I could now work towards. I didn't know any trauma surgeons nor did I know the steps needed to take towards becoming a doctor, but I was determined to get to work on making my new-found dream a reality. I had discovered a ferocious drive to succeed because I had now attached my success to something bigger than myself – my community.

In order to make strides towards achieving my goal of becoming a doctor, there were several challenges I would need to overcome. I grew up in a single-parent home on a council estate in Peckham – one of the most deprived areas in South East London. Most of the young people I grew up around did not have aspirations of becoming a doctor or studying at university. I wasn't aware of anyone within my family or social network who was a doctor or had ambitions of becoming a doctor. I met my biological father for the first time when I was 19 years old which meant I didn't have the guidance or affirmation from of a father figure growing up. Out of my four siblings, only one other went to university – that was my elder sister, Annette. Pursuing higher education was not the common culture in my family but knowing that my sister had been to university meant the prospect of it was not so alien to me. My mother was only educated to GCSE level and she left high school with no qualifications so she was not sure about how to navigate the higher education system. Although my sister was not familiar with the process of applying to medical school, her knowledge about the overall university application process definitely offered some guidance. In the first instance, I didn't even realise that these were huge obstacles. I'm naturally an action-orientated person – when I decide I want something, I always ask myself, "What is the next move I need to take to make this thing happen?" In this instance, I decided that I would do some research. I simply opened up my laptop and did a Google search on the steps I would need to take to become a doctor.

After doing so, I realised that the first step I would need to take, would be securing strong grades for my GCSEs. Most medical schools wanted students who were scoring As in most of their GCSE subjects. I decided that I would challenge myself by setting the goal of 10 A stars! I was motivated to set such an ambitious goal because, as well as having a head teacher who encouraged us to aim for As, there were two German sisters who each achieved straight A stars in their GCSE subjects. The elder sister achieved 13 A stars and the younger 14.5 A stars. These two sisters were visible examples of what was possible! I remember reaching out to the elder sister to ask if she could help me with my French homework. She kindly agreed and I met her about two or three times in the school library to go over French. Although we only had a few sessions together, these encounters inspired me to pursue academic excellence. Setting the goal of 10 A stars was a challenge that intimidated me, but one I was willing to rise to. I reassured myself that even if I did not meet this goal, that falling short would most likely still secure me pretty good grades.

Furthermore, I promised myself that no matter what grades I achieved, I would be proud of myself for putting my all into working towards my goal. Having such a clear vision about what I wanted to achieve for the future became a turning point for me in my academic journey. Although I have always been gifted with intelligence, I have not always applied myself which meant I sometimes fell short of my true potential. Below are some extracts from my year 8 school report which demonstrate this:

"Leanne is a spontaneous, hardworking and determined student. She works hard, but unfortunately, she also talks a lot. I believe Leanne could do even better if she talks less and keeps focused during lessons, this will give her more chance of her attaining her target level."

"Leanne is not working as well as last year. She allows herself to be easily distracted and this is sometimes affecting the quality of her work. When she focuses on the set task, she displays good skills and produces quality work. Unfortunately, her website project was incomplete, but she attempted most of the skills and achieved quite well in the task. Overall, Leanne has just met the requirements for level 5 and will need to work determinedly to consolidate this level and to progress in order to meet her target level."

"Leanne attends P.E. on time and in full P.E. kit. She clearly enjoys the subject but must learn to control and channel her energy. She finds it difficult to concentrate and at times is off task. For example, running around the court rather than completing the task or talking to friends. To improve her performance, she needs to ensure she always listens and carries out instructions promptly. This in turn, will improve her overall level of effort and participation in lessons."

As you can see from the above extracts, I was not the most focused student, and this lack of focus was affecting my attainment. However, this all changed when I decided that I was serious about working towards becoming a doctor. My academic success became of great importance to me. After reasoning in my heart that achieving 10 A stars was the goal I was committed to working towards, I started living a very structured lifestyle. I had a study timetable that I kept to. There were days when I was bored and tired of studying, however, the vision I had for my future was motivation enough to keep going. I am a strong believer that when you have a powerful *why*, it gives you the self-discipline and tenacity to consistently drive forward towards your goals.

Your *why*, in simple terms, is the thing in life you're passionate about, the thing you're committed to, the thing that fuels a fire in your heart. Often times, a person's *why* is born out of adversity. You'll find that people who are very passionate about a particular cause, are often the same people who were once victims of what they're fighting for. For example, someone who is a strong advocate for persons with disabilities, might have a disability themselves, or know someone close to them who has a disability. Being able to experience or witness the challenges a person with a disability face, gives them an empathy and compassion which drives them to action. This is because, when you have a personal experience with something, it often leaves an imprint on you that serves as a constant reminder of why you are passionate about the thing you are. Maya Angelou said it perfectly in her famous quote: "People will forget what you said, people will forget what you did, but people will never forget how you made them feel." For me, my *why* was linked to my community. I was aggrieved by the fact that young black men were losing their lives over matters so seemingly trivial. I wanted to make a difference and the only logical idea I had at the time, was the idea of becoming a doctor. This was my *why*, this was the fuel that burned a fire in my heart that simply would not go out. Having such an emotive *why* meant that when I came up against obstacles, when I felt like giving up, when I was tired of revising; I would remember why I was doing all of this in the first place. I would remind myself of my vision and my desire to positively impact my community. This mental exercise often gave me the strength to be consistent with my revision and to stay focused when the temptation to go astray knocked on my door.

One of the key principles I was very good at practising, is the principle of delayed gratification. Delayed gratification is the act of postponing immediate pleasure so that you can enjoy long-lasting pleasure. For me, this meant I would sometimes say no to social activities, like going out with my friends, so that I could revise. I reasoned that performing well in my GCSEs so that I could increase my chances of achieving my overall dream of becoming a doctor, would be more pleasurable to me than enjoying the immediate gratification of socialising with friends. This is not to say that I became a total hermit. It is very important to have social interaction and to make time for rest and relaxation, but I planned this. By planning this, it helped me to make sure I was getting the right balance between having fun and working consistently towards my goals. I vividly remember a situation where my commitment to delayed gratification was tested. It was a really sunny day, something that is a rarity in the UK, and my friends were all planning on going to the park to enjoy the weather. I was part of a group chat where they were discussing their plans for this, however, according to my study schedule I needed to revise history. History was one of the subjects I found more difficult to revise for because although I enjoyed writing the essays, I used to find it quite challenging to read through the material needed in order to write the essays. I recall looking down at all of my history books, and then looking out of my window at the sun. My heart yearned to go to the park with my friends to enjoy the sun in their company, however, my wisdom told me that I needed to prioritise my history revision since my exams were fast approaching and I had an academic goal I was working towards. As such, I decided that I would forgo the trip to the park. I encouraged myself that in summer, I would be going on a family holiday where I would be able to enjoy unlimited sun!

Despite the background I was coming from, I received a lot of support along my journey. My secondary school teachers were immensely helpful. One of the things I've learnt along my journey, is that when people notice that you're serious about achieving a goal, when they see your determination and focus, they are often willing to help support you! My teachers were very impressed by the focus I had and so they were willing to give me their time and offer me extra support. One of the subjects I found quite challenging was maths. However, I was determined that maths would be one of the subjects that I scored an A star in. As such, I gave a lot of time to revising maths outside of school. My teacher noticed an improvement in my understanding of maths and she also noticed my determination to achieve. I asked her for past exam papers and she would print them for me. I then spent several lunchtimes in her office where she would willingly work through the answers to the questions I hadn't answered correctly. She noticed how much effort I was putting into my studies and because of this she too, wanted me to succeed. When people, be it your teacher or a mentor or someone in a position above you, can see that you are really trying hard to succeed in something, they will often want to help you to win! Do not be afraid to reach out to mentors to ask for extra support. I have never been shy about asking for help and I believe this is a key characteristic that has helped me to succeed along my journey.

Chapter 2

First Steps Towards My Dream

During my final year of high school, my sister suggested that I apply for a Sixth Form bursary or scholarship. A scholarship or bursary covers the cost of a student's education at an independent, fee-paying school. They're usually awarded on the basis of academic attainment or some other kind of achievement e.g., playing competitive sports. My sister's suggestion for this was inspired by a memory she had of a student in her high school who had been awarded a scholarship for Sixth Form. In fact, my sister told me that this student did not have a very good experience, which wasn't a great selling point to begin with. Apparently, she dropped out not long after because the school she went to was run like a military camp. She would have to wake up early to march around the school with the other students. This, of course, did not sound very appealing to me. However, my sister reassured me that different private schools operated differently and ideally, I would apply for ones that did not run like military camps! She explained to me that if I applied for a scholarship this could be a very valuable opportunity for me as it would provide me with a good quality education and access to many opportunities and resources that a state sixth form might struggle to provide, or simply not have access to. My sister's reasoning seemed very logical to me. Besides, I have always been very fond of my sister and respected her advice. She was one of my earliest role models and she played a very significant role in my education. She was the reason I studied at the high school I did. When I was 11 years old and thinking about the high schools I would apply for, she did research to find out which schools were the best in the area and together, we went to many of the open days. She played a very active role in my educational journey and career aspirations. Throughout high school she would attend many of my parents' evenings, alongside my mother. However, my sister understood the education system in a way my mother did not. My sister would ask the teachers questions at my parents' evenings to help make sure I was best placed to thrive. My mother recognised that education was important and she supported me as best as she was able to.

She would never hesitate to buy me any books I needed for school and supported my extra-curricular interests. In addition to this, my mother never once told me I could not achieve my dreams. She always used to refer to me as "the A girl" and she was convinced I could become anything I wanted to be. I could have told my mother that I wanted to build a rocket to space and she would have never said it was impossible. Having a mother who did not doubt me, was a great source of encouragement for me.

As mentioned earlier, my sister attended most of my parents' evening alongside my mother. There is a vivid memory I have from one particular parents' evening, that has never faded away. We were in the main hall where many of the teachers for different subjects were seated at different desks spread out inside of the hall. Before joining the queue to visit one of my teachers, we paused at the Head Girl board. This was a wooden board which hung on the wall and listed the names of Head Girls dating back to at least 50 years ago. My sister gazed at the board, and then she paused to look down at me. I looked up to her and she said to me "Leanne, one day your name will be on this board." After my sister said those words to me, I remember feeling a mixture of fear and inspiration; but mostly fear. The thought of being head girl terrified me. You see something I had always struggled with is public speaking or being in the spotlight. The role of head girl inherently involved both of these things. Despite feeling scared at the thought of this, I recognised what an amazing achievement it would be if one day it could be me. Deep down, beyond the feeling of fear, there was a part of me that would have loved the opportunity to be Head Girl and have my name engraved in the wooden board forever. Well…four years later when I was in the final year of my high school, my sister's words came to pass as I was chosen to represent the school as Head Girl. I was overjoyed and pretty surprised at the announcement! Partly because I was in the "naughty class" and I clearly remember my head teacher once reprimanding my class, she yelled, "There will never be a head girl from this class!" Well, they say never say never right?! Even though this honour had been bestowed upon me, the reality is that I still felt that terror inside that I felt the four years prior when my sister and I looked up at the Head Girl Board. I did my best to speak whenever I was called upon, but the truth is, I lived the entire year as head girl struggling with anxiety. For the first ever speech I gave, I remember leaving the stage feeling completely humiliated. I was asked to speak alongside a year 7 student and I was more nervous than her! My hands shook violently as I read from a piece of thin paper and my heart raced inside of my chest. After the speech one of my "friends" told me that I looked as if I were "dancing on the stage" because my body was shaking. These words cut me deeply as I knew public speaking was my fear and her analysis of my performance reinforced this fear. In spite of this, deep down, I had a strong conviction that there was a powerful voice inside of me. I had always believed that my life's purpose would involve public speaking, specifically inspirational speaking. I loved to inspire my friends to dream of bigger than what they could see, both within themselves and in their surroundings. As such, after each speech, despite battling humiliation, anxiety and fear, I often felt a sense of accomplishment because I knew I had challenged myself to do something that I was born to do. One of my teachers reassured me that by the end of the year I would become a much more confident speaker. I held onto these words. I did develop as the year progressed but I was still far from a great speaker. However, by the end of the year, I did feel confident enough to start volunteering for public speaking opportunities in the future. Being able to develop the confidence to do this was of crucial importance because it greatly helped me along my journey to becoming the inspirational speaker that I am to date.

During my final year of high school, I heeded my sister's advice and I decided to go ahead with applying for a scholarship or bursary. One evening we sat at my laptop and researched various private schools which offered bursaries and scholarships for their Sixth Forms. We ordered a number of prospectuses from various schools. When they had eventually all arrived in the post, we sat down on my bedroom floor and together we read through the prospectuses. In all honesty, I had little motivation to read through pages upon pages of text, I simply browsed through the pictures. After doing so, I decided that Mill Hill seemed like the Sixth Form to apply for. For each application made, there was a fee of approximately £100 and so we decided that I would only submit one application, that being Mill Hill.

A few months later, when I had almost completely forgotten about the application we had made, I received an invitation for interview in the post. By this time, I had already experienced a few interviews from the local Sixth Forms I had applied to. Nonetheless, I still felt quite anxious about the Mill Hill Interview because it would be very different from all the other Sixth Form interviews. At Mill Hill I would have several interviews with different members of staff, including a maths test which made me feel particularly nervous as maths wasn't my strong point. As I normally did, and continue to do with anything that makes me feel nervous, I prayed about it. I prayed that God's will would be done; that if it was His plan for me to study at Mill Hill School I would, and if it was not His will I would not be offered a place. When the day to be interviewed finally came, I decided to wear my school uniform to the interview. Initially I was planning on wearing something smart but the idea came to me that if I wore my school uniform, which had all my badges of achievement on it, one of the interviewers might ask me a question about my badges. This would then be a prime opportunity for me to talk about the various leadership positions I had been appointed.

When my sister and I first arrived at Mill Hill School, we were taken on a tour around the school. I remember marvelling at the scenery around me. The beautiful buildings, the green landscape, the fact that the school had a swimming pool! I had never seen a school like this before. When it came to my round of interviews, I remember having to leave my sister for most of them. I felt very nervous about it but I tried my hardest to remain confident and to do the best I could in each interview. I found the maths interview particularly challenging. I remember being invited into a room where I sat directly opposite a maths teacher, we were separated by a small square table. On the table lay a sheet of paper with maths questions that she asked me to answer. What I worried might happen, indeed came to pass – I had a moment of jelly brain. It felt so nerve wracking having someone stare at me as I tried to solve maths problems. My brain just stopped working. She was a very lovely woman, she encouraged me that if she was in my position, she too would feel very nervous and then she began to give me clues to help me work through the maths questions. Following this interview, I had an interview with the head of Sixth Form. My sister was allowed to join me for this interview. I remember feeling quite fond of the head of Sixth Form, she was a very bubbly and talkative lady and there was something that felt very motherly about her. The final interview of the day was with the headmaster of the school. Together my sister and I went into his office and I remember looking at the grandeur of his filing cabinets which stood directly behind the sofa on which he was seated. I remember the headmaster greeting us with such warmth. He asked me about my ambitions and somehow, I remember us discussing the topic of Africa. I spoke passionately about how one day I would love to contribute to making positive changes in Africa. He asked me if I were to be offered a place at Mill Hill, how I would make the most of it. I remember telling him that I was determined to get involved with all of the activities the school had to offer and that I would make the most of the experience. In addition, out of all of the interviews I had, it was during the headmaster's interview that he noticed my uniform blazer decorated with badges. He asked me what the different badges were for and I was able to tell him about my role as Head Girl and school prefect. He was particularly impressed by this and of course, I was totally chuffed because my plan of wearing my uniform with the intention of discussing my badges worked!

On my journey home I remember feeling good about my short, but activity-packed, trip to Mill Hill. It was an experience like nothing I had ever had before. My sister shared the same positive feeling I had and we agreed that God's will would come to pass – if I did not secure a place at Mill Hill I would have lost nothing, and if I did secure a place then it would be an amazing opportunity for me.

A few months after my interviews at Mill Hill, I received a letter from the school. I had already reasoned in my mind both possible outcomes and concluded that neither would be too bad. Despite this, I still felt quite nervous before opening the letter. If the letter was a rejection letter, I would feel disheartened to know that I did not make the cut. After all, who likes to be rejected? If the letter was an acceptance letter, I would now need to mentally prepare myself for the new journey I would embark on. Deep down inside it was my desire to study at Mill Hill. I knew it would be an amazing opportunity, something I ordinarily would never be able to afford, and I believed it would act as a stepping stone towards achieving my dream of becoming a doctor. I was also prepared to do anything that would help me draw closer towards my dream of becoming a doctor. I eventually opened the letter and I remember being completely blown away by what I read – "We are delighted to offer you the 100% ABC bursary to board at Mill Hill." Wow, it was actually going to happen! The fantasy I had imagined in my mind of what living at school would be like would no longer be a fantasy. I remember telling my teachers at school the news: to my surprise I received mixed responses. Some seemed really chuffed for me but others seemed a little more sceptical. I remember one teacher telling me that, "Now you're going to the other side of life." I just smiled in response, I had no idea what she meant by "the other side of life" and I didn't bother asking. Another teacher warned me about the "snooty" environment I would be entering. Another teacher was quite disappointed that I was choosing to board over going to my high school's Sixth Form, especially being Head Girl. Despite this, there were other teachers who were very pleased for me. Some told me that I would now have so many great opportunities and that I should take full advantage of this. In all honesty, I was not completely sure what to think or feel about this new journey that I would embark on. I knew it was a very valuable opportunity, and for this, I was determined to make full use of it. I told myself that no matter what challenges may lay ahead, it would only be for two years and all I needed to do was keep my goal of getting into medical school at the forefront of my mind. I trusted that God would be with me every step of the way; encouraging myself in this way gave me great comfort and confidence.

Now that I knew I had been given such a great opportunity for my Sixth Form education, I was all the more determined to excel academically. I totally committed myself to my studies. I had a routine I followed – I would go to school, come home, eat dinner, rest a little, then study until it was close to bed time. I did this Monday to Friday, and on the weekends, I would also try to incorporate some study time in. I had clarity over what I wanted to achieve and as such, I was committed to doing everything I could to increase my chances of reaching my academic goals. Once I had completed all of my examinations, I felt a great sense of relief. I had worked so hard towards them so to finally be able to have a break from my vigorous revision schedule was liberating! Eventually, results day drew closer and closer until the actual day arrived. I remember feeling terribly nervous on results day. I knew that whatever I scored I needed to be proud of myself because I had put all my effort into preparing for these exams; however, in spite of that I was still nervous. I had a goal I was working towards, an academic target I was hoping to achieve and results day would be the unveiling of whether or not this goal had been met. I remember going to my secondary school with my mother to collect my results. I refused to open the envelope which concealed the paper with my results. I wanted the moment to be private when I read my results. As such, I waited until I reached home and then I went straight to my room and sat on my bed. I prayed a lot before I finally plucked up the courage to open the envelope and read the paper. When I read my results, I was utterly amazed! I had actually achieved my goal; I had secured the 10 A stars at GCSE that I had been working so diligently for. I was totally blown away by this achievement and indeed, it felt like a miracle to me! I remember ecstatically typing an email to the head teacher at Mill Hill to share the good news with him. He, of course, was very impressed by my efforts and he congratulated me and told me the school was very much looking forward to me joining.

Now that I had completed GCSEs, thoughts about going to boarding school filled my mind. What seemed like a distant endeavour, was now closer than ever before. I had chosen to study History, Mathematics, Chemistry and Biology for my first year at Sixth Form. A few weeks into the summer holiday before I would start Sixth Form, I was mailed a suggested reading list for History. I ordered some of the books and started reading them, however, I was struggling... Struggling to grapple with the material I was reading. This made me feel quite insecure as I knew that I needed to achieve As at A level in order to study medicine. I persevered with the pre-reading and just reassured myself that somehow everything would work out...

Chapter 3

Boarding School

Just like that, summer was over and my first day of boarding school had arrived. I was nervous, but I felt ready. It was about a two-and-a-half-hour drive to the school from my home. I felt anxious throughout the entire journey and I wasn't sure what to expect. However, I had been pondering this moment for months now and so I was as mentally prepared as I could be. Once I arrived at the school my headmistress greeted me. She was a lovely woman with a very warm presence. She made me feel very welcome and reassured me that I'd be okay. She showed me to my boarding room which was on the third floor of the boarding house. It was a reasonably sized room that I would share with another student. I wasn't too keen on sharing a room with someone I did not know. We both had our own single beds which were positioned parallel and separated by a reasonable amount of space. There was a window in our room through which you could see the garden; it was a beautiful view and I found it quite calming. I began unloading my suitcase and stacking my new shelf and everything started to feel more real. I would now be living at school for the next two years; all for the purpose of working towards my goal of securing a place at medical school so that I could become a doctor.

The boarding house I lived in was predominantly male, there were about 40 students living in the house in total, and of those, about eight were female. For the most part, I developed good relationships with all of the boarders, however, there was one particular character that I struggled with. He noticed that I was different and when he learned that I was from South London, he became very intrigued by this and would often make quite condescending remarks. For example, instead of calling me my name, he would often refer to me as "badman". His perception of South London was largely based upon what he read and saw on social media or in the news and he was projecting many of these stereotypes on me. He would often question me. Some of his questions included, "Have you seen anyone get stabbed before?" and "Are you on a bursary?" If I am honest, I felt quite insecure about being on a bursary. Although it was something to take pride in, I often felt like I was being judged negatively for it. People would often ask me questions – both students and teachers – because they knew I was from a different background to them. These questions sometimes felt a little interrogative...as if they were trying to decode my socioeconomic status and my background in general. I understand that people can find it quite interesting when they come across someone different from themselves, but when you're at the receiving end of it, it can make you feel a little alien. Although this was challenging and it made me feel quite insecure, in retrospect I am grateful. Through this experience I was challenged to look introspectively and ask myself deeper questions about my identity. I did not choose the environment or the family I was born into and neither does anybody else. We are all dealt different cards in life and we have to choose how to handle these cards. We can choose to walk in self-pity about all the things we do not have, or we can choose to work with what we have in pursuit of creating the life we want. I was choosing the latter.

I quickly adjusted to life as a boarder. Besides living on site, the only other major difference was having school on a Saturday morning. I boarded from Monday to Saturday, meaning I went home every Saturday afternoon and returned back to my boarding house on Sunday evenings. The boarding community was made up of three separate houses of mostly international students. Many of them were from China, Russia and Germany. I found comfort in that I did not have to catch a plane to see my family members, I just needed to take a few buses and a train. I cherished returning to South London on my Saturday afternoons. I loved going home to sleep in my double bed, to see my family and to go to church on Sunday mornings. In fact, I probably looked forward to church more than I did anything else. My faith has, and continues to, form an integral part of my journey. As a boarder I needed to adapt to a new routine. For example, we had midweek and end of week assemblies in the lounge area of the boarding house. These assemblies definitely made it feel like I was at school in the evening! However, I soon became accustomed to my new routine and began to really enjoy several aspects of boarding. For example, as a boarder I had access to the school grounds in the evenings for various activities. I would often exercise at the school gym or go for a midweek swim in the school pool. There was also an evening lecture series that we could go to. I particularly loved the lecture series as sometimes they would have fascinating speakers. We once had a talk from Professor Derek Yellon, an internationally renowned cardiology expert. He spoke about some research he had been involved in linked to delaying the death of cardiac tissue during a heart attack. I will never forget this experience as it was absolutely fascinating! To hear a lecture from one of the world's leading figures was a moment that felt like the world had opened up for me. I too, started to think about the possibility of being internationally renowned for the work I would one day do in my own field of specialty. Experiences like this inspired me and expanded my belief in what was possible for myself.

There were other perks to boarding school that I enjoyed. Living on site meant I could wake up later as I did not have to worry about a long commute. I also had breakfast, lunch, dinner and lots of snacks available to me so I never had to worry about cooking. The school environment was beautiful – there was a lot of greenery and occasionally I would explore this on a run. I met some wonderful people, some of whom I am still friends with today. There was a particular border called Josh who had a great influence on me. He was a fitness fanatic and would often go on long runs around school and in the local area. I would sometimes accompany him on these runs and his passion for fitness re-ignited mine. In addition to this, he had an exceptional drive. Once he put his mind towards something, nothing stopped him! He would drive at his goals like a bull and as a result he would achieve exceptional results. Perhaps he reminded me of myself! Josh also studied chemistry and sometimes we would revise together or work through homework together. Being able to study in the evening with your friends was a particular advantage of being a boarder that I relished. I would sometimes struggle with my maths homework and many of the female boarders were also studying maths, some further maths, and so they were very useful for helping me solve maths problems.

During my first year of boarding school I studied Biology, Chemistry, Maths and History. Each subject challenged me in a different way and I needed to work very hard to keep on top of my grades. During my lunch breaks I would often go to my teachers to ask for their help with the areas I was struggling with and after school I would set aside a few hours each evening for revision. As well as working hard academically, I made a great effort to get involved in extra-curricular activities as I knew this would be very important for my application to medical school. I was involved in the swim team, the philosophy club, cadets, and occasionally cross country. I also managed to secure various work experience placements. I worked exceptionally hard to make myself a competitive medical school applicant. After my first year of Sixth Form, I managed to secure the grades I needed to apply for medical school – you needed a minimum of 3 As and one B, which were exactly the grades I achieved. I applied to four different medical schools and a fifth back-up course which was biomedical science. Shortly after applying for biomedical science, I received a notification confirming that I had successfully been offered a place. However, I was not interested in studying biomedical science so this didn't excite me. Months passed before I heard back from each of the medical schools I applied to. The first medical school I heard back from did not give me good news – they rejected me without an interview. This was a hard pill to swallow but I reassured myself that there were three more medical schools to hear from. The second school I eventually heard back from also rejected me without an invitation to interview. This felt like a second blow, but again, I reassured myself that there were two more schools to hear back from. The third medical school I eventually heard from also rejected me without an invitation to interview. By this point, I started panicking. I needed to start thinking about a back-up plan. "What if the final school also rejected me? What would I do? Would I take a gap year and reapply to medical school hoping I would be successful on second attempt? Would I accept my backup offer?" These are the multiple questions that shot back and forth across my mind.

I finally heard back from the final medical school, several months after submitting my initial application. People often say the phrase "no news is good news" and so I had hopes that the delay in hearing back from this final school could be testament to this. However, when I opened the notification to read this university's response, to my devastation, it was bad news! My final hope for getting into medical school had been zapped away as they too, informed me that they had rejected my application to study medicine. I felt heartbroken… I had poured everything into trying to make myself a competitive applicant and it almost seemed as though my hard work counted for nothing. In addition to this, I felt like I had let others down. I had a range of mentors who were all rooting for my success and hoping for me to eventually become a doctor. I particularly felt I had let Mill Hill down. I was the first recipient of their *A Better Chance* bursary, a bursary specifically for a student who wants to study medicine or dentistry. Despite the school never putting overt pressure on me to succeed, I wanted to make them proud. I wanted their investment to be worth it! After the initial sting of this disappointment started to subside, I began to think more deeply about what my options would be. I had received an offer for the back-up course of biomedical science but this was not good enough for me… I did not want to study biomedical science, I wanted to study medicine! At times, I can be quite a stubborn character and this was one of those moments where I did not want to budge. I wanted to give myself a second chance. As such, I decided that I would reject the back-up offer of biomedical science and reapply to medical school the following year. This felt slightly risky because it meant I needed to secure a minimum of 3 A grades in my A-levels in order to reapply. Although I have excelled academically, it has never been a straightforward journey for me. It sometimes takes me longer to grapple certain concepts and so I was not over-confident about my ability to achieve these grades. However, my faith in God and my deeply rooted conviction that it was my purpose to become a doctor, gave me the mustard seed faith to take this risk.

Over the course of my second year of Sixth Form I worked my backside off! I studied relentlessly and held onto the hope that my dream of getting into medical school would someday become a reality. Since I was planning to reapply to medical school, this meant I would need to take a Gap Year. I was not certain about what I would do during this year but I knew that I would be able to figure something out. As the end of my second year of Sixth Form was drawing to an end and exam season was approaching, my nerves began to heighten. Along my academic journey a mindset I have held onto which has helped me in the midst of anxiety is the belief that so long as I do my best, my best is good enough. I reassured myself of this as I sat through each exam paper, however, there was one particular paper that left me feeling deeply disappointed. It was my final maths exam… Maths was one of the A-level subjects I found particularly challenging. During the exam there were questions that I was completely unsure about. Unlike History or English, you do not have the liberty of trying to put together words that sound logical and broadly relate to the question. Maths is black and white, though there are several methods you can use to work toward the same answer, for the most part you know if your calculations are logical or if they are totally off track. For much of the paper, I was convinced that I was totally off track. I have never been one to cry after an exam, but this exam pushed me over the edge. It was my final exam and I was convinced I had screwed it up. It felt like the weight of my destiny was carried by this one exam and I had blown it! After the exam I walked straight back to the boarding house. I did not stop to discuss the paper with any of my peers, in fact I never discussed exam papers after I had completed them. For me, these discussions often made me feel anxious or worried as they would make me question most of the answers I had written. On reaching the boarding house I went straight to the girls' common room; this was a very small room on the female floor of the borders' house, it was often a free space you could sit in. Once I reached the room I sat on the floor, faced the radiator and cried into the palms of my hands. It was all I could do. I had so much emotional tension built up inside of me and I had no idea what lay ahead. I just knew that I wanted to become a doctor with all that was within me and I was uncertain about whether or not this dream would come to pass. I had heard about alternative routes for gaining places at medical school, such as graduate entry programmes, or conversion courses; but they were not what I wanted. I wanted to get into medical school first time round, I wanted the certainty of knowing that I would eventually become a doctor!

As I had just completed my final exam, this meant my time at Sixth Form was drawing to an end and I would embark on my gap year. I managed to organise a range of activities that would keep me busy and productive. I was determined to make the most out of the year and I am too much of a busy body to lounge around. As such, I worked as a lifeguard, I volunteered as a support worker for Doctors of the World, I volunteered as a speaker for Asthma UK, I volunteered for my friend's charity Revive Congo and I did a small amount of travelling. This gap year turned out to be an incredible year and I am so grateful I had the opportunity to take it. Sometimes life takes us on detours, I felt like I was on a detour because in my mind the perfect plan would have been that I went straight to medical school from Sixth Form. However, sometimes it is the detours that provide us with the most amazing opportunities which allow us to grow and develop in ways we might have not otherwise. As a support worker for Doctors of the World, I helped vulnerable people such as undocumented migrants, asylum seekers and victims of sex trafficking, access GP services. As an 18-year-old, this was the first time I had interacted so intimately with people facing these kinds of issues. In my makeshift consultation room, some of the service users would share their stories with me. Many of them had been through horrific experiences that are difficult to even imagine, let alone comprehend. This was an invaluable learning experience that would serve me well, both as a doctor, and for my own personal development. The experience taught me that life is not black and white! Before volunteering for Doctors of the World I had never imagined that there were people living in London who were in dire situations and needed access to healthcare but were struggling to do so. The experience opened my eyes up to the harsh reality that some of the most vulnerable members of our society face. This humbled me and it taught me the importance of being even more compassionate, non-judgemental and kind to the people I meet in everyday life, and especially to my patients.

During my gap year I had the opportunity to travel to India with a charity called Free the Children. I was there for 21 days, the longest holiday I had been on. I travelled with a group of about 20 young people – we had all been awarded a scholarship, sponsored by Virgin, which funded the trip. We were selected based on our leadership skills and desire to make a positive difference to our community. The purpose of the trip was to further cultivate our leadership skills and to support some of the local communities in Northern India. We were there to learn about their culture and the challenges they face. It was a valuable opportunity that hugely inspired me and empowered me with the mindset that I have the ability to create change! It also reminded me of how blessed I was to have been born in the UK with the plethora of opportunities we have here. Above all, it served as a positive distraction because at the start of my gap year I was still waiting to receive my A-level results. After my summer exams, there were about three months I would need to wait before results day. These three months felt like the longest three months of my life and it was an extremely challenging period for me emotionally. I felt like I was in a limbo land, like my destiny depended on a piece of paper which would list my three A-level results for Maths, Chemistry and Biology. I had poured everything I had into preparing for my A-level exams, as well as preparing myself to be a strong medical applicant. As an aspiring medical student, there are a range of tick boxes you need to meet which extend beyond securing the right grades. You need to develop your communication skills, your critical thinking skills, your leadership and team working skills; and the list goes on… I had prepared myself the best I could and now, all I could do was wait patiently for my results. Worrying about them was not going to speed up time, all I could do was wait and hope for the best. I contemplated the prospect of not achieving the grades I needed and having to reorientate my life's compass. However, this was not what I wanted! I did not want to follow a plan B; a plan B was not good enough for me! I wanted my plan A to succeed, I wanted to gain a place at medical school! My deep yearning to gain a place at medical school, challenged by the prospect of not meeting the entry requirements became an internal conflict that caused me to feel quite low over the 3 months I had to wait for my results. My coping mechanism was hope. Despite all my doubts I just hoped that somehow everything would work out. I continued to believe that all of the investment I had made in myself and others had made in me, was not in vain. I held onto the hope that God has a plan for my life which included me becoming a doctor. I tried to encourage myself with the hope that no matter what happened, somehow it would all work out. A great source of encouragement for me during this season of my life was Benjamin Carson's book *Gifted Hands*. It outlines his journey and his struggles, his hope in God and even some of the miracles God performed in his life. As a student, I felt a deep connection to Ben Carson's story and his struggles. He was my virtual role model. Though I had never met him in person, his books gave me insight into his journey which I found great comfort in.

On the day I returned to the UK from India, all I could think about was my results. It felt as if my destiny lay in an envelope. My desire to study medicine was the strongest desire I had for anything at that time. I was obsessed with doing everything I could within my power to make it a reality and I was now about to find out if my results would permit this. I remember knocking on the door to my home and my sister answered. We greeted each other and the first thing I asked for was the results envelope. My sister handed me a brown paper envelope and with a deep breath I nervously opened it in front of her. On the results paper I saw 3 As and I fell straight to the floor in disbelief. I was over the moon, absolutely ecstatic, filled with excitement and a renewed sense of hope for my future. Now I had the A-level grades I needed, this would make it so much easier for me to apply to medical school and everything inside of me believed that I would be a successful applicant on this second round of applications.

On applying to medical school the second time round, I secured interviews for three out of the four medical schools I applied to. I had always believed that if I had the opportunity to have an interview, I would stand a good chance of gaining a place at medical school because I'd be able to demonstrate my passion and commitment. My prediction was correct because I secured offers from each of the three medical schools where I had been interviewed. I was absolutely ecstatic! Of the three medical schools, I decided that I would study at St George's University of London. This was largely because I wanted to remain living in London.

Chapter 4

Breaking Boundaries

On my first day of medical school, I remember feeling a mixture of emotions – anxiety, excitement, fear, apprehension, doubt, hope and gratitude, to name a few. I remember thinking, *now I have managed to get into medical school, how am I going to get through*!? Despite my apprehensions, fears and insecurities, I continued to hold onto the hope that all would be well. My dream was manifesting itself and the prospect of actually becoming a doctor was closer than ever before! My first year of medical school turned out to be a great year. They gently eased us into the course and I was able to start developing my new revision routine whilst also getting involved in some of the extracurricular activities on offer. Forming new relationships was something I focused on during the first year. I fondly remember meeting a medical student called Grace, who was a few years above me. Grace really inspired me because she was a relatable role model who was excelling academically. She was a young black woman who I felt more culturally connected to compared to most of the other students at my medical school. I remember once overhearing Grace in a corridor as she spoke about her achievement of 1st decile in her recent exams. Unlike most degree courses, medicine is marked based on deciles. You pass or you fail and within the pass mark there are 10 deciles, with the top 10% of the cohort scoring 1st decile and the bottom 10% of the cohort scoring 10th decile. Grace was testifying to a friend that she had achieved 1st decile, so she had scored amongst the top 10% of her year. When I heard this, I remember being amazed and filled with awe. To see a young black woman who did not look like the stereotype of a nerd and yet was excelling and walking in confidence filled me with pride for her and massively inspired me. If she could do it, so could I! I remember speaking to Grace about how much she inspired me and she became a mentor of mine. She encouraged me that I too could excel academically and she was happy to offer my peers and me teaching and guidance throughout our medical school journey. Grace also became the trigger to an amazing idea I developed which changed my life in ways I could have never imagined.

I was on holiday in Malta and Grace and I were messaging through WhatsApp. I asked her what she had been up to and she mentioned she had been featured in the Future Leader's Magazine – a magazine that highlights 150 of the UK's most outstanding African and African Caribbean students and new graduates. What an amazing achievement I thought and I congratulated her for it. I mentioned to her that I would love to also be featured in this magazine but at that time I did not feel that I was demonstrating any authentic form of leadership. Grace responded, "Well now is the time to start!" These words hit me in a very profound way! I thought, *now really is the time to start*! Filled with a new sense of enthusiasm, I went back to the hotel room that evening thinking, *what can I do to demonstrate my leadership skills in an authentic way*? Then an idea came to me! During my first and second years of medical school I was one of my university's student ambassadors. As a student ambassador, you had the opportunity to take part in "taster weeks" and other types of programmes which were designed to give students, particularly from under-represented backgrounds, an insight into the world of medicine, so as to inspire them and increase their likelihood of pursuing higher education. As a student who was coming from an under-represented background – both in terms of my ethnic background and socioeconomic background – I felt very passionate about these types of programmes. One of the disappointing realities was that despite these programmes being present, there still remains a significant lack of diversity across UK medical schools – most medical students come from wealthy backgrounds and have family members who are doctors. This offers them a significant advantage when it comes to applying to medical school and being successful. As I sat in my hotel room in Malta, my thoughts raced through my mind as I searched for an authentic, and meaningful way I could display my leadership potential. Eventually, an idea came to me! I decided that I would develop my own medical outreach programme that would help to level the playing field by offering students from under-represented backgrounds the support they needed to become successful medical applicants. I reasoned in my mind that as a student coming from an ethnic minority and a disadvantaged background, I had special insight into the challenges students from these types of backgrounds face. As such, I wanted to design a programme that would address these challenges and in doing so, help students overcome these challenges so that their dreams of becoming a doctor were not halted by factors they have no control over – such as their race or socioeconomic background.

I remember discussing the idea with one of my friends called Aharoun. He loved the idea and said he believed that I was on to something great. Together we brainstormed a name for the programme and he suggested it could be called the "Leanne's

Amazing Medics' Programme". I shared his idea with some of my other friends and mentors and they loved the name and said it had a ring to it. As such, I decided to run with this name. The Leanne Amazing Medics' Programme was designed to be a six-session programme delivered over a course of six months. Each of the sessions were designed to inspire, equip and increase the self-confidence of the students who partook in the programme. The sessions would be part theory and part practical, giving students the opportunity to implement the skills they had learnt. Now that I had brainstormed my idea and created a preliminary programme, I reached out to a mentor, named Veronica, and told her all about my idea. I asked her if she would be able to offer me guidance so that I could transform my idea into a reality. Veronica was just as excited about my idea as I was! She said that she would be delighted to support me in the manifestation of this idea and we arranged a meeting. Veronica advised me that I should write "a case for support" in preparation for this meeting. I had no clue what a case for support was and so I told her this. She explained to me that it was a written document which, in simple terms, should outline who my organisation is, what we do and why we do it. I would then be able to share this document with prospective donors or other organisations that might be interested in supporting my work. I followed Veronica's advice and created this document and when we met up, together we sifted through the document and she offered suggestions for how I could improve it. I took notes and later that evening I started implementing her suggestions. In addition to the case for support, Veronica advised me that the next step would be piloting my programme. Filled with excitement and fear, I started brainstorming how I would make the pilot work. I decided that I would firstly reach out to my former high school's sixth form. I emailed an old teacher and told him that I would love to deliver a medical outreach programme to his Sixth Formers in the hope of inspiring them to pursue their dream of becoming doctors. He loved the idea and was very welcoming. We secured dates in the diary for when the programme would take place and he advertised the opportunity to the students. Eight students signed up for the programme. I also reached out to my university's medical education department and asked if they'd be willing to loan me equipment that I could use as part of the sessions, and they agreed. In retrospect, I recognise this was quite a blessing as they trusted me with ECG machines, first-aid manikins and other types of medical equipment that they would allow me to take off site.

I felt extremely nervous as I was trotting along with this idea. I was worried about whether the students would engage, if the programme would be worth it, and if I was taking on too much alongside my studies. However, above all of these doubts in my mind, there was a stronger voice which was compelling me to run with my idea. I focused on the purpose for why I was doing it – it was to encourage students coming from similar backgrounds to myself, that they too could be successful in becoming doctors. I wanted to be a visible role model and I wanted to empower them that they could make their dreams a reality! I reasoned in my heart that even if they decided they didn't want to become doctors, as long as my programme had empowered them with the self-belief to know that they can achieve their potential that alone would be worth it.

Now that I had secured a Sixth Form and had a planned programme of content I would deliver, the next step was to find some volunteers. I shared my idea with some friends at medical school and asked if they'd be willing to get involved. They loved the idea and were very happy to offer their support. This allowed me to form my first team of volunteers and together, we successfully delivered the pilot programme. We had a great time engaging with the students and teaching them new skills. They also expressed their enjoyment and testified of how much they were learning from the programme, and how much their self-confidence and ambition for the future had increased. On evaluating the pilot programme, although it had definitely had a positive impact, I realised that the intervention would be more effective at achieving its overall objective if it targeted a younger audience. This is because by Sixth Form, the students we were targeting often hadn't chosen the right subjects or they hadn't secured the grades or work experience they needed. As such, we agreed that the intervention should start earlier with year 8 and 9 students. Around this time, we also submitted an application to my university for some funding to assess the impact of the Leanne's Amazing Medics' Programme. Our grant was accepted and this allowed us to expand our delivery to two additional schools. As the number of schools we worked with increased, our team of volunteers also increased. During this time, I also connected with a friend, Daniel Huf, and told him about the programme I was running. He loved the idea and seemed just as passionate as I was. He said he would be keen to get involved and we started working together before eventually become co-founders. Together we transformed the programme into a fully registered charity called The Armitage Foundation. Daniel isn't from a medical background; he studied English literature at Cambridge and then entered into the world of consulting. As such, he was able to bring great strategic insight which helped us to take what was the Leanne's Amazing Medics' Programme working in three schools, and convert it into a fully-fledged charity which is currently working with seven schools, is partnered with two universities (King's College London and St George's University of London) and Medway hospital. The

Armitage Foundation, is committed to building a long-term continuous intervention which will be able to support students from year 8 all the way up to their application to medical school in year 12. We are building three programmes called Armitage Juniors (formerly known as Leanne's Amazing Medics), Armitage Seniors and Armitage Scholars, which follow on from one another. This long-term, continuous intervention means we will be able to support students at all the critical time points along their journey towards applying to medical school. It also gives us the time to cultivate the seed of inspiration that is planted through our first programme, by further building upon the skills and tools the students have learnt. We believe this approach will best position students from under-represented backgrounds to be successful medical applicants.

What started off as a medical outreach programme in my old secondary school's Sixth Form has become what I never imagined. It's allowed me the opportunity to connect with amazing individuals from all walks of lives. It's taught me the power of collaboration and working with a team to build something greater than yourself. I have been invited to give speeches sharing my journey and highlighting the importance of increasing diversity across UK medical schools. I've featured in multiple media outlets including the national news, national newspapers and national radio stations. It's resulted in me receiving numerous leadership awards including the 2018 UK Queen's Young Leaders award, presented to me by Her Majesty the Queen at Buckingham Palace. This was one of the greatest moments of my life so far because it encapsulated everything I stand for. As I stood before Her Majesty, I just remember thinking, *what are the chances of this? That I, Leanne Armitage, from a single parent home on a council estate in Peckham would go*

*on to meet Her majesty the Queen at the tender age of 23, whilst
still a medical student?!*

For me, this was a living, breathing example that
irrespective of your background you can create a great future for
yourself. That determination, focus, resilience, commitment and
refusal to be swayed by life's setbacks goes a long way! People
often ask me, "Leanne what was it like meeting the Queen?" In all
honesty, I struggle to put it into words. On the day of the
ceremony there were about 60 other young people waiting to
receive awards. I was one of the final delegates who would go up
to receive the award. I remember watching the Queen stand and
interact with every person she presented an award to. I thought,
*surely, she is going to be too tired to speak to me when I go up to
receive my award.* However, I was pleasantly surprised. After I
curtseyed and walked towards her to receive my award, she shook
my hand and then said to me, "You were the girl in the video
weren't you?" At the beginning of the ceremony, a short film was
played which highlighted the work of some of the people being
presented awards and I was featured in this video. I was so
surprised that the Queen had recognised me. I told her that it was
me and she encouraged me to continue my good work. It was a
beautiful experience and I am so grateful to have photos and a
short video which captured the moment.

I want to end this chapter by encouraging you to hold
onto your dreams and persevere. Throughout my journey thus
far, I've constantly had to battle with the emotions of fear,
timidity, insecurity and doubt. As you choose to step out of your
comfort zone and challenge yourself, you'll inevitably experience
uncomfortable emotions. One of the key principles that has
helped me to subdue these negative emotions is focusing on my
vision and focusing on my *why*. My vision, meaning the image I
visualise of what I hope to achieve for the future and my *why*,

meaning the purpose which ultimately drives me. I'm driven by a strong desire to impact the community and world around me. When I see an issue I feel deeply about, I start to think about potential solutions and then I feel a compulsion to go to work on creating these solutions. By having a clear sense of what it is I want to achieve and why I want to achieve it, this has helped to provide a strong driving force which helps me to keep persevering in the midst of intimidation, doubt and insecurity. I would also often reassure myself by asking the question, *what is the worse that could happen*? Even if I "fail" at a venture or project I commit myself, I hold strong to the mindset that I would rather try to make a difference and fail, than to not try at all. After all, with trying there is a chance of success, compared to not trying at all which guarantees no success. A powerful secret I have also learned along my journey is that there really isn't such a thing as failure. Failure is all about perspective. In every single situation there is an opportunity to learn – whether that be learning how something can go well or how it can go terribly wrong. Both are equally valuable lessons and if you can interpret negative or unexpected situations as learning experiences and use them as a springboard to move forward, eventually you'll often find yourself landing in a place of success. People often allow their apparent failures to suffocate their dreams and steal their hope for the future. If you can start working on building and developing the resilience to learn from failure and continue persevering towards your goals, I'm confident you'll eventually bump into success.

Part II

Seven Principles to Help You Achieve Your Dream

Chapter 5

Principle 1 – Creating Your Vision

In order to achieve a dream, you first need to have a dream.

Occasionally in life you may stumble your way into success, but more often than not, you have to be very intentional about achieving the goals you set for yourself. Distractions surround us, and so unless we're intentional about pursuing a particular path, there is a high likelihood that we'll be side-tracked, knocked off course, or hindered by obstacles along our path. One of the key tools you can use to help lead a life of intention and clear direction, is a vision board. A vision board is a visual representation of the goals and dreams you have for the future and it can take several forms. For example, you could create a collage of different images, you could draw a picture, or you could even write a collection of words or sentences which affirm the life you want to live. There are a variety of different ways you can create a vision board, but ultimately, the end result should be a visual representation of the dreams you have for the future. A vision board is powerful because it acts as a constant reminder of what you're working towards. It gives you clarity over your end goal and in doing so, helps you to focus on the bigger picture. This helps to prevent you from becoming caught up, or distracted, by the minor details. For example, if one of the goals on your vision board is to pass your driving test, the specific details surrounding the day of the week you practise driving or the specific driving school you use, are not as important as the overall goal of passing your test. When you focus on the end goal, the question to ask yourself becomes, *will taking this step help me to reach my overall goal* rather than *should I drive on Saturdays at 9am or Fridays at 6pm*? Driving on a Saturday morning versus a Friday evening will definitely impact your driving experience in that the Friday rush-hour traffic may mean you're spending more time than usual waiting in queues of traffic as opposed to practising driving. However, the overall point I am trying to make here, is that when we focus on the small details, we can sometimes delay our progress even further. Even if on a Friday evening you're driving for less time than you would on a Saturday morning, if you're consistently driving on a Friday evening, you are still going to make progress towards your overall goal, albeit, at a slower rate. Life's circumstances will never be perfect and there will always be an excuse or a seemingly logical justification for why you should delay something or leave it all together. It's therefore important that you develop a mindset which does not easily leave room for excuses. Focus on progress over perfection. As long as you're progressing in a forward direction, even if the circumstances are less than ideal, overall, you're still on track towards achieving your vision.

Creating a vision board does not need to be a difficult or laborious activity. It is something you could complete in 10 minutes or you could choose to spend the entire day on it. How much time and effort you put into creating the vision board is your choice. The ultimate goal is to have a visual representation of your future goals. Creating a vision board is also not a one-time activity. With time, your ideas about the future life you want to live may start to change and as such, you may want to adjust your vision board to accommodate these changes. Some of you might have a clear mental image of where you want to be in one year but not in five years. Some of you may say I only have a clear image of where I want to be in 3 months' time. This is completely fine. So long as you have some idea of the direction you want to travel in, you can create a vision board. Let me offer you an example to help make my point; most people would agree that having good health is important to them. With poor health come a host of different challenges that can limit you and prevent you from walking in the freedom you would hope to enjoy. As such, most people would be open to the suggestion of having something on their vision board which represents a healthy body and healthy mind. Similarly, most people would agree that financial security and stability are important. Who likes the threat of feeling financially unstable, not being able to provide for yourself or your loved ones? Most people would therefore agree that having something on their vision board which represents financial security would be a good idea. With these two ideas alone, you could create a vision board with two images – one that represents good health and the other that represents financial stability. Once you have created your vision board, you then want to place it somewhere where it is easily accessible so that on a daily basis you can look at your vision board. By repeatedly looking at these images every day, they are becoming embedded in your subconscious mind and will therefore have the power to begin influencing the daily decisions you make. Throughout the day when you're making food choices, or deciding on whether to take the bus or walk, your decisions will be influenced by the image of good health you reminded yourself about in the morning. Even if you're making poor decisions related to your health, you'll have an increased awareness of it which can help to form a boundary preventing you from going beyond a certain limit. It can also encourage you to try again the next day! In the same manner, if you're at work and you are getting frustrated by your job, the image on your vision board which reminded you about financial stability will encourage you to be grateful for the job that you have, since it offers you finances, and in addition to this, it may also inspire you to pursue a job that you will enjoy more and that will pay you more. It may even give you the courage to pursue your own business venture. To change your life from where you are to where you want to be, it starts with your thinking. You have to think differently to achieve different results and a vision board could be the catalyst which helps you to change your thinking, and thereby change your life, by encouraging you to take steps closer towards achieving your dream.

Although a vision board can be a great catalyst for helping you to achieve your goals, a vision board alone is not enough. It is important that you clearly define your goals and create a feasible plan which can take you from where you currently are, to where you want to be. For example, if you have an image on your vision board that represents health, in order to make strides towards being the healthiest version of yourself, you will need to think in more detail about what this means for you. Do you need to lose a specific number of kilos in order to be a healthier weight? Once you have a clearly defined goal, you can start creating your plan of action which will allow you to materialise your goal. For example, on the same topic of losing weight, you can ask yourself the following questions which will help you to create specific action points: How many times will you exercise per week to reach your target weight? What types of exercises will you do? What kind of diet will you eat? How many calories will you aim for each day? Unless you think about your goals in detail and come up with a suitable plan of action for realising your goals, you will either delay your progress or prevent yourself from achieving your best. As such, your vision board becomes a tool that needs to be supported by a more detailed plan of action in order to bring it to pass. At this stage, people can start to feel overwhelmed because it can seem like the workload is too much. The idea of this exercise is not to make you feel overwhelmed, however, naturally you will feel uncomfortable as you set goals which challenge you to be and do better. The important thing to remember is that you can break these goals down into bite-sized chunks and you can slowly increase your effort as you start to become more comfortable with your new habits and routines. For example, if you set the goal to exercise four times a week and normally you do not exercise at all, this is a very ambitious goal that initially would be a shock to your system. The way to slowly ease yourself into something that initially might seem too difficult, is to start small and slowly build yourself up. Commit to exercising once per week and work at being consistent with this before you introduce a second exercise session into the week. Once you're consistent with doing two exercise sessions per week, you can then continue to build yourself up until you're hitting your target of four exercise sessions per week. When you take things step by step, these small efforts start to compound over time and before you know it, you begin seeing great progress. I would encourage you to practise reviewing your progress at regular time intervals e.g., every three months. You may find that you have soared in some areas and struggled in others. The areas where you've struggled could be a result of trying to progress too fast, if this is the case, you can slow down your speed and set more realistic goals. In contrast, it could be that you need a different, more suitable strategy. In the following chapter I will focus on implementing the strategy needed to help achieve your dreams.

As briefly mentioned earlier in this chapter, you have to be very intentional about achieving your vision so that you're not thrown off course by the various distractions and obstacles life may bring your way. As humans, something we all struggle with from time to time is exercising our will power and walking in discipline. We are often challenged by what we feel like doing versus what we know is the right thing to do. For example, if a warm, freshly baked chocolate sponge cake dripping with chocolate sauce is offered to us, many of us would find it difficult to say no. However, if you know that one of the priorities on your vision board is good health or to lose a certain amount of weight, you can more easily resist this temptation because you're focusing on your overall vision versus the momentary pleasure of the enticing cake. A vision board highlights your priorities, and it helps you to make daily decisions that are in alignment with your future goal. This allows you to develop habits that are in alignment with your dream. As a result, you begin moving from where you currently are to where you want to be. As well as being able to resist temptation and say no to things that will take you off course, you need to be able to recognise great opportunities and say yes to the things that will take you closer to where you want to be. Knowing what to say yes to is equally as important as knowing what to say no to. When a great opportunity comes our way, there may be a number of factors which make us question whether to accept or reject the opportunity, "Will I have enough time? Am I skilled enough? How will the opportunity benefit me? Will the work required be worth it?" are a number of questions we may ask ourselves. A vision board can be pivotal for making big decisions as you can ask yourself, does this opportunity line up with the overall vision I have for my future? If the answer is yes, the return on investment may be more clearly visible to you, motivating you to take the opportunity with more certainty and less doubt. By the same token, if the answer is no, you can have greater conviction in your decision to say no which will help avoid feelings of guilt or second-guessing yourself.

A vision board can be a powerful tool for developing resilience. The journey towards success is not a walk in the park, it comes with a fair share of ups and downs. During the down moments, we can become frustrated, tired, demotivated and question if it is all really worth it. Having a vision board can serve as a spring board, helping you to bounce back from these low moments. This is because a vision board reminds you of your *why*. Your *why* is the driving force behind your vision. It is the reason why you are passionate about achieving your goals. When you can strengthen the power of your why, you are much more likely to steadily ride through the lows and blaze through the highs. Your *why* serves as a deep conviction within your heart which is not swayed by the ups and downs of your emotions, or changes in your external circumstances. Your *why* stands firm in its belief and it anchors your heart to your dream. Your *why* can adjust and evolve with time, as you learn more about yourself and the world, but its purpose remains the same. To give you an example, in the earlier chapters of this book I shared my story with you. I spoke about how my desire to help address the issue of knife and gun crime within my community inspired me to aspire to become a trauma surgeon. This was my *why* – I was aggrieved by the brutal and untimely death of young men over seemingly trivial issues and I wanted to change this. My *why* was something that I was deeply connected to at a heart level – it was something that triggered an emotional response inside of me when I thought about it. As such, when the setbacks came, such as struggling with my academic journey, being rejected from medical school, and doubting my ability to achieve my dream, my *why* prevented me from throwing in the towel. I had attached my vision to something greater than myself and so when I thought about the prospect of giving up, there was more on the line than just the abandonment of my own dream… To give up on my dream, meant to give up on my community. My dream of becoming a trauma surgeon gave me the hope that I could be a part of the change I wanted to see. The thought of giving up on this hope in the face of challenges was not an option for me. I was set on achieving my goal of becoming a doctor and I was determined to do everything within my power to make it happen. It's been over ten years since the incident which sparked my dream and the honest truth is, right now I no longer have the ambition of becoming a trauma surgeon. However, this is not because I have abandoned my dream, it is because my dream has now evolved. With time and experience I have learnt more and seen more and realised that there is more I can do in areas that are better suited to my character, skills and passions. I still have the activist spirit I have always had and I still do care about the issue of knife and gun crime, but I've also developed new passions along my journey. Now I am focused on changing the landscape of the NHS medical workforce through my charity The Armitage Foundation. Working to increase diversity across UK medical schools feels more aligned with my purpose in this season of my life.

We all have a *why*, we have all had experiences which have triggered us and ideas which have entered our minds for what we could do or the part we could play in the world around us. Sometimes fear prevents us from feeding our *why* and believing that it is possible for us to achieve our *why*. However, you ultimately have to make the choice as to whether or not you will allow fear to swallow your dreams. Fear is something that will never stop trying to challenge you but the more you challenge it, the more you develop the strength to walk in courage, which means to stand up in the face of fear. I want to encourage you to reflect on your life and the idea that you have a purpose. That you have a unique set of skills, talents and passions that can be used for good in the world around you. I want to encourage you to do a little soul searching and to think about how you can contribute to the world around you in a meaningful way. When you're able to identify what you can do and you begin walking along this path, you develop a sense of fulfilment like none other.

Chapter 6

Principle 2 – Developing Your Strategy

To give feet to your dream, you first need a strategy.

A strategy is plan of action to help you achieve your goals. This plan is carefully crafted so that it is in alignment with the specific goal you want to achieve. A strategy is important because no matter how intense your desire is to accomplish something, desire alone does not make it happen; you need to act! Your strategy forms your action plan so that you can take the necessary steps to turn the idea in your head into a reality. Creating your strategy is just as important as executing your strategy because if your strategy is in misalignment with the goal you're working towards, chances are you won't achieve your desired result. You may still make progress and learn along the way, but it's unlikely you'll reach your intended goal. To offer a practical example, the strategy one might implement to become an aeronautical engineer is not the same strategy one would need to become a doctor. There may be aspects which are similar, but they are not the same. A strategy is not a one-size-fits-all formula; you need to be careful to develop the right strategy for you.

To create an effective strategy plan, it would be a good idea to start with some background research. By researching you'll be able to develop a broad understanding of the steps needed to achieve your goal. For example, if your goal is to become a doctor you need to understand what the academic requirements are, what the admissions tests for the universities include, what extra-curricular activities are important and what work experience you might need. Getting the research part right when creating your strategy plan is very important. If your strategy is informed by the wrong information, you may take the wrong steps which will inevitably lead you in the wrong direction. To avoid being misinformed, carefully consider the sources you seek to inform your strategy plan. I would always advise you to start by finding someone who has excelled in the area that you are hoping to excel in. If they have podcasts or online material that you can listen to, submerse yourself in it. Or better yet, if you can arrange a meeting or phone call with that person, do this. Through speaking with them or listening to their material, try to understand their journey and the steps they have taken to get to the place where they are. Once you begin understanding the strategies they used, you can begin emulating them. In your process of researching, I would also encourage you to investigate several sources as this will help you find what is best suited to you. In addition to this, it will also help to give you a balanced view of what the necessary steps may be. People will have different opinions and different preferences and if you base your strategy plan on only one source of information, this might be biased. Seeking a range of sources allows you to balance out these biases and to create a plan that is well suited to your preferences. This is important because the better your strategy plan is catered to your character, the higher the chances are that you'll succeed. For example, I have never been someone who works well at night time, I like to go to bed early and rise early. Some of my peers, particularly at medical school, would prefer to study throughout the night because that was the time when they were able to have optimal focus as distractions are minimal when most people are sleeping. However, this strategy would not work for me because as I said, I like to sleep through the night. Being able to seek counsel from a range of people and a range of sources allows you to consider and weigh up different perspectives, ultimately allowing you to decide what the most suitable plan of action will be for you.

Once you have crafted a strategy you are happy with, you then want to create a timeline so that you can work towards a deadline and identify the key time points along this. This is a very important step because there may be time-specific goals that you need to meet. For example, if your goal is to study a particular course at university there may be specific interview dates in the admissions process. If you have an idea of the time these interviews will take place, you can make sure you set aside sufficient time along your timeline to ensure you're well prepared for these interviews. Planning things in this way allows you to avoid the last-minute flurry that comes with a lack of preparation. After you have formed your timeline, it would then be a good idea to highlight the key milestones, or the key events along that timeline. Once you've identified these, you can then start breaking down the necessary action points to meet these key milestones. Once you've identified these action points, you can then start working on them in bite-sized chunks. Carrying out this process helps you to take what may seem like a huge and daunting goal, and break it down into manageable steps which you can work on day by day. Having a timeline which has key milestones included also allows you to monitor your progress against these milestones which helps to give you an idea of how on track you are towards your goal.

When creating your strategy towards your goals, it is important that there is some flexibility. Unexpected things in life happen and in the face of these surprises, you might not be able to stick to your initial strategy plan. You can pre-empt and plan for some challenges, and I would advise you to do this where you can. However, there are some challenges that may be totally unexpected and, in these situations, you most likely will have to completely adjust your strategy at that point in time. The beauty of having a vision board is that it keeps you centred. Even if you need to totally change your strategy plan, the ultimate goal remains the same which will help to redirect your strategy.

In my pursuit to becoming a doctor, my strategy was interrupted when I was rejected from every single medical school I applied to. My initial strategy involved applying to medical school during my final year of Sixth Form and receiving at least one offer which would allow me to start medical school the following academic year. However, this strategy would no longer work and as such, I needed to return to the drawing board. In doing so, I decided that I would reject my back-up offer of biomedical science and take a gap year and reapply to medical school, in the hope of being successful on second attempt. This was based on the presumption that I would secure the grades I needed in my final exams. I knew I was taking a risk and I was willing to do this because I believed that my act of faith (rejecting my back-up offer in the hope I'd secure the grades I needed to reapply to medical school), would act as a driving force, motivating me to work hard enough to secure the grades I needed. I also had to research other options in the event that my plan B did not work. In this scenario, I could either reapply for biomedical science at a university that offered a transfer to medicine course or I would need to complete the biomedical degree and then apply for graduate entry medicine. This is an example of how there are multiple routes to achieving the same goal. For me, the direct route was the most convenient route but even if that route didn't work, it would not be the end of my dream.

People often give up on their dream when they encounter a diversion that sets them off track, especially when they've worked exceptionally hard in the hope that their initial plan would work. The reasons why people give up on their dreams are numerous and often vary, but one thing I have noticed is that the hurt of rejection can prevent people from trying again. It knocks their confidence and makes them question their ability to achieve their dream. I wish people discussed, or were asked about their setbacks, as much as they are asked about their successes. You would find that many successful people have experienced their fair share of setbacks but they tried again and in doing so, were eventually successful. Thomas Edison is a principal example of this; in his pursuit to create the lightbulb he failed 10, 000 times, but he did not allow these failures to define him. He had a winner's mindset and so eventually, he won! In an interview, when asked how it felt to fail 10 000 times, Edison responded, "I have not failed 10,000 times—I've successfully found 10,000 ways that will not work." Being able to cultivate an attitude and mindset of resilience, which I like to define as the ability to bounce back from life's set-backs, will help you to be more flexible with your strategy plan and adjust it, rather than terminate it, in the face of a challenge. Edison is a fantastic example of the power of doing just this! What I love most about this quote, is his perception of the failures as successes – they were successful in showing him how not to make a lightbulb. You often find that you learn some of the greatest lessons and experience great character development through life's setbacks and seeming failures.

Once you've received clarity over your strategy, you need to focus on executing your strategy. No matter how excellent and well thought out your strategy is, unless you go to work on executing it, in essence it becomes meaningless. To consistently execute will require stamina, focus and discipline. You need stamina because it's not a sprint, it's a marathon. It is the work that you do on a daily basis that will compound over time and draw you closer to your vision. Some of the practical tools you can implement to help you execute your strategy include having a schedule. On a Sunday, you could create a timetable of the week ahead and plan your activities for each day, with your end goal in mind. Other people prefer to create daily to do lists with the key activities listed first on the list. The specific tool you use does not matter, so long as you are mindful of the key areas you need to work on, and you set aside time to go to work on these things. At first, a task like this can feel very laborious and somewhat pedantic. However, it is very important that you push through these emotions because ultimately, you are trying to create a new habit here – a habit which requires you be very disciplined and intentional about how you use your time. This is when refocusing on your vision board becomes so important, because it is the excitement and passion you have for the overall vision that will inspire you to commit to the seemingly laborious and pedantic activity of planning your week and your individual days. Once you start developing these habits, they become more natural to you and you begin to action out your priorities without putting too much thought into them. For example, health and fitness is a very important part of my life. I set the goal of working out at the gym four times a week and I always meal prep for the week ahead. As such, on a Sunday, in my mind I will agree on the four days of the week I will go to the gym. I also know that on the weekend I must find a two-hour time slot to commit to meal prepping for the week. Since these are routine activities I do, it becomes much easier to action these priorities because they have now become a part of my routine habits.

One of the key things you can do to help you remain committed to your strategy plan, is having an accountability partner. An accountability partner is someone who holds you accountable for the goals you want to achieve. They are very useful to have because they offer an additional layer of support which means your journey towards your goal is not in isolation. When you know someone has agreed to invest their time and effort into being your accountability partner, in the face of challenges when you may feel like slowing down or giving up, knowing that someone else is invested in your success acts as a deterrent to this. Furthermore, you can share some of the challenges you are facing along your journey with your accountability partner who can act as a sounding board and a source of encouragement for you. The relationship you have with your accountability partner and how often you check in with them will depend on what you agree and it is a good idea to have an initial discussion with them so that you can set out expectations. Having an accountability partner is not the only form of holding yourself accountable, sometimes it can be a simple act such as making a public declaration. A public declaration may sound quite lofty, but this could simply be telling three friends that you want to lose 10kg and you're committed to working towards this. There is something powerful about sharing your intentions and goals with other people. Whenever you do this, it subconsciously puts pressure on you to work towards achieving this because you have now shared the goal with others who may well ask you about your progress towards this goal in the future. However, similar with creating a strategy plan, you have to find the type of accountability that works best for you. For some people, making a public declaration would not be a good idea as it could result in them feeling an unhealthy amount of pressure, such that in the event of not achieving their goal, they feel a deep sense of shame, disappointment, and failure. This is not the goal of accountability. You want there to be a healthy amount of pressure that pushes you towards achieving your goals and helps you to maintain consistency in this pursuit. You may have days when you go off track, or you slow down, or you pause; and that is okay! But ultimately, the purpose of accountability is to help you move in an overall forwards direction so that you can reach the goal you have set out to achieve.

As well as having an accountability partner, there are practical tools you can use to help you effectively carry out your strategy. For example, you can use the Eisenhower matrix to help you triage your to-do list. The Eisenhower matrix helps you to identify and differentiate between what is important and urgent, important and not urgent, not important and urgent, and not important and not urgent. Below is a visual example of this matrix:

	Urgent	Not urgent
Im po rta nt		
N ot I m p		

Ideally, you want to focus most of your time and energy on the top two boxes in this matrix – the urgent and important activities and the not urgent and important activities. This is because your urgent and important activities are key to your overall progression and they have a time frame attached to them which offers a deadline you need to work towards. Your activities that are not urgent and important do not have a time-frame attached to them but they still need to be prioritised because they are the activities which will help you to draw closer towards the vision and goals you have for the future. To offer a practical example, an important and urgent activity might be a presentation you need to deliver at work in the following week. This presentation could have a large bearing on your professional development and as such, it becomes an urgent and important activity. A not urgent and important activity could be your goal to exercise three times per week. This is not urgent in that, by missing an exercise session overall, it is not detrimental. However, it is important because exercising three times per week will have a large bearing on your overall and long-term health. In contrast, a not important but urgent activity might include deciding to go to the shopping mall for the final day of a sale for clothes items that you don't need, but would be nice-to-haves. And finally, a not important and not urgent activity might include buying some extra teabags so that you have a stock, even though you currently have more than enough teabags.

Creating a matrix like this may seem like a simple activity you're tempted to pass on by, but I encourage you to give it a try! You'll be surprised by how much mental clarity an exercise like this can offer you, but allowing you to visually differentiate your priorities and therefore highlight the areas that are important for you to focus on.

THE POWER OF A DREAM

Chapter 7

Principle 3 – Mindset

The manifestation of any dream starts in the mind.

Your mindset is of crucial importance on your journey towards achieving your dream. Your reality is a reflection of the thoughts you have about yourself and the world around you. Your thoughts influence your decisions, which influence your actions, which start to form your habits and then ultimately, your daily habits shape your reality. In order to take yourself from where you are now, to where you want to be, you need to start with your mind. You need to go to work on developing the daily habits that are in alignment with your vision as where you will be in 3 months, 6 months or 10 years from now, is to a large degree shaped by your daily actions. A good starting point, is to ask yourself the following questions:

Do I have the mindset that will allow me to make the decisions that will take me to where I want to be?

Do I believe I am worthy of success and the dreams I hope for?

What limiting thoughts are slowing down or preventing my progress?

What can I do to create the mindset that will help me achieve my dreams?

It is really important that you be honest with yourself as you answer these questions. They will offer you a good starting point in relation to figuring out how aligned your thoughts are to a success mindset. People are often trying to manifest the fruit of success without planting the right seeds and providing them with a healthy environment to grow. Your mind provides the environment that will either cultivate and nurture your dream, or cripple and diminish your dream.

When I decided that I wanted to become a doctor, I needed to go to work on changing my mindset. In the early stages of my journey, I struggled with insecurity, low self-esteem and doubt that was contending with this dream. I used to ask myself, "Is it really possible for me to realise the life I dream of when no one in my environment, no one on my council estate, has done this before?" Is it really possible for me to challenge the status quo? Is it really possible for me to be what I cannot see? At this point I was 15 years old and so I had little power to change my physical environment – I couldn't move out of my council house to an environment where success was normal and people were thriving. I was a teenager, dependent on my mother to shelter and look after my basic needs. However, I realised that I could create my own mental environment which could empower me to achieve my goals irrespective of my physical environment. I detached myself from the poverty, the stereotypes and the limitations I saw around me by empowering my mind with podcasts, sermons books and various other content that would inspire me to dream big. I would write words of affirmation and powerful declarations on sheets of paper and stick them around my wall. I positioned them in visible places so that I could read them on a daily basis and by doing so, change my thoughts so that they were now in alignment with my dreams. My mind slowly started shifting from a place of limitation, doubt and insecurity, to a place of hope and confidence in my ability to realise my dream.

Along your journey of changing your mindset, you may have experiences or encounters that may set you back or expose an area of weakness that you need to work on. Even though these experiences may feel negative, they actually provide really powerful learning opportunities. To give you an example of one of my own experiences of this, as mentioned at the beginning of this book, I was awarded a bursary at a private boarding school for my Sixth Form education. With this opportunity came an extreme shift in my physical environment. I transitioned from living in a council estate in a deprived area to a large boarding house, amongst students from very successful and wealthy families. With this extreme shift I had my first encounter with imposter syndrome. Often imposter syndrome is self-inflicted, in that the people around you do not regard you as less than able or not up to the mark, but you feel this way. However, in my case, I felt like my experience of imposter syndrome was being reinforced by some of the people around me. For example, many of the students and teachers were aware I was on a bursary and some of them would ask me personal questions about my background which would make me feel very uncomfortable. I felt like I was being judged negatively for differences I had no control over. Whether or not this was true, I will never know, but what I do know is that feeling like an impostor and feeling like you are not completely welcome in an environment where you want to thrive, is a very challenging experience. For the entire duration of my Sixth Form journey, I struggled with this feeling despite working on my mindset to empower myself. I say this to encourage you that the journey of transforming your mind is a process. Thinking like an imposter will limit your ability to express the fullness of who you are, but when you can recognise these negative thought patterns you can begin challenging them. In doing so, you can prevent yourself from making decisions from the paradigm of an impostor. For example, if feeling like an imposter would make me feel nervous about pursuing a certain opportunity, I would remind myself that I am just as worthy as anybody else and then I would challenge myself to pursue it. Being able to recognise and challenge your negative thought process is critical because the reality is, along your journey towards pursuing your dream, you will question yourself. You will encounter experiences that make you feel uncomfortable and, in some cases, people may even express their overt disapproval of you. However, you have the power to rise above this negativity. You can go to work on strengthening your muscle of resilience and empowering yourself that you are worthy of the positions and places you find yourself in, and any that you wish to pursue.

One of the key things that has helped me along my journey of transforming my mindset, and continues to help me, is finding and connecting with identifiable role models. People who had achieved similar things to what I hope for and who I feel I can relate to on a personal level. Hearing or reading their stories fills me with hope and further fuels my drive to achieve my dreams. My first, profound experience of this was when I came across Dr Ben Carson's book *Gifted Hands*. I read this book during my first year of Sixth Form and it changed my life. Whilst I was at Sixth Form, I often struggled with self-belief. Deep down, I believed it was possible for me to become a doctor; but there was an internal battle which caused me to question myself. At Sixth Form, I was surrounded by students who came from wealthy and successful backgrounds. My inability to relate to this made me feel isolated at times and caused me to doubt my own potential. However, through reading Ben Carson's book; for the first time in my life I was able to connect with a story I could relate to. Ben Carson was a black man who came from a single parent home with a mother who had a limited education. In spite of this, he had a dream of becoming a doctor. Not only this, but he experienced a turbulent academic journey. He went from being called the class dummy to then being awarded scholarships, including a scholarship to study at Yale – one of the most prestigious universities in America. Furthermore, Ben Carson's faith was a fundamental part of his journey, as is mine. Learning all of these facts about Ben Carson and being able to relate to him on these multiple levels was a profound encounter for me. It filled me with such great hope that I could achieve my dreams; that even if my journey was not as straightforward as I hoped, it would somehow all work out and I just needed to persevere. A relatable role model can be such a great source of inspiration; however, the unfortunate reality is that there are not always relatable role models in the positions we hope to find ourselves. Sometimes, we are the very person blazing the trail along a path that may have never even been walked before! As such, it is important that you go to work on developing your self-confidence. When you are confident in who you are, and you are confident about the dreams you have for the future, this will help you to push boundaries and achieve things that others have never done before. Developing this confidence can take time but it starts with identifying the limiting thoughts you have in your mind and working on challenging these. It starts by empowering yourself and being your own personal cheerleader. Sometimes, even those close to us, who love us and want the best for us, can discourage or sway us from pursuing our dreams. This is why developing self-confidence is so important. When your dream defies the expectations and logic of those around you, it is your confidence in yourself and your dream which will empower you to rise up and keep driving forwards in the face of such resistance. Everyone's path is different in life, but I'm confident that there is no emotion or pressure that is new to mankind. There are many giants who may not have walked the same path as you, but they've experienced very similar challenges. They were able to overcome and so irrespective of the pressures you may face, you too can overcome.

Part of the journey of developing self-confidence involves accepting yourself for who you are, and choosing to love yourself. Sometimes we can be our own worst enemies because we judge ourselves harshly for things we had little or no control over. You cannot control the background that you come from, you can only accept your circumstances and choose to move on from them. In the same manner, you should not hold yourself captive to past mistakes or past negative experiences. You have to choose to let things go that do not serve to take you to where you want to be. You have to accept that some of the decisions and choices you made in the past that you may feel ashamed of, were a result of the limited knowledge you had. Now that you have more knowledge and self-awareness, you can choose to be and do better. Accepting who you are and choosing to love yourself is key to unlocking the greatness that resides inside of you. We all have a unique set of characteristics, a unique personality and a unique set of talents; when you can focus on developing these, you will excel! Sometimes because we are so focused on outside distractions and what others are doing, we try to emulate others and we fail. This is because we are trying to be something that we were never designed to be. It is of utmost importance that you understand yourself, your own passions and your own purpose and begin focusing on these. You can only be the best version of yourself, not somebody else. If you are someone who has not yet discovered their purpose, I encourage you to spend time thinking about this. You may not find the answer straight away, but if you start asking yourself questions such as, "What am I passionate about? What part do I want to play in the world? What triggers or makes me angry? What natural skills and abilities do I have? What do I enjoy?" you'll start to slowly develop more clarity over the areas of life you should focus on, and eventually, you'll develop a clearer understanding of your purpose.

We live in a society that teaches us to do the opposite – it encourages us to focus on other people's lives, to desire what others have and to aspire for unattainable standards of beauty, for example. It is great to be inspired by others and to celebrate the success of others, but you should not focus on others so much that you lose sight of the beauty that lies within you. You have to steward your own gifts and not allow yourself to become distracted by focusing on the gifts of others. To work on developing a healthy mindset it is a good idea to have a daily practice that cultivates self-confidence and self-empowerment. This needs to be a daily practice because, similar to fitness, once you reach a goal you're happy with, you have to be consistent with the disciplines that will enable you to maintain that level of fitness otherwise you'll begin to lose it. Having a daily practice which edifies your mind helps you to challenge the daily negative messages that are being thrown at you and allows you to focus on what is important. Practically, some of the things you can do to help develop and maintain the right mindset include having a morning routine. Checking the news, emails, or messages first thing in the morning is not the best way to start your day. Oftentimes, the news has negative information and reading messages or emails that remind you of tasks you need to get done is not the most empowering way to start the morning. Listening to a podcast or some kind of inspirational content can help to kick start your day in a positive way. Exercising first thing in the morning is also a great way to start the day as the endorphins and various hormones released offer you a natural high. Personally, my morning routine involves prayer and positive affirmations. I like to either look at my vision board, or look at myself in the mirror and make declarations about my day and my future. Starting my morning in this way acts as a consistent reminder of the end goal which helps me to stay motivated when I start becoming tired of what can feel like the day-to-day mundanity of routine life. A morning routine can vary from person to person, but ultimately, the purpose is to start your day from a place of empowerment because the outlook you have at the very start of the day will filter through the rest of your day.

The final point I want to touch on concerning mindset, is the importance of have a zero-tolerance attitude for negativity and toxicity. We're already exposed to a level of negativity that we have little power over e.g., we cannot control what we'll see on the daily news, the challenging colleagues that we may work with, natural disasters, or public health catastrophes such as the Covid-19 pandemic. As such, it becomes all the more important to limit or if possible, completely mitigate, your exposure to the negative influences that you can control. Sometimes this can be challenging because it may be family members or people that we feel a sense of loyalty to, but it is important you prioritise your own mental wellbeing. I've often heard people say that their greatest critics and enemies of progress were those closest to them e.g. family members or former friends. Someone's negative or doubtful voice concerning your dreams for the future or the current trajectory you're on can serve as a distraction from what you're doing. It can cause you to question if you're on the right path and if you have the capability to succeed in your pursuit.

Anyone who truly cares for you should not intentionally make you feel this way. Sometimes your loved ones might disagree with what you're doing, but their feedback should come from a place of love and constructive criticism, rather than destructive criticism. A negative influence in your life does not always have to take the form of a physical person, it could be a TV programme you're exposing yourself to, or a genre of music you're listening to. We may not think much of these things in the moment, but if you are repeatedly listening to a negative message over time, it will begin to influence your mindset and outlook. Your outlook will impact your decision-making process and therefore your actions, which as we discussed earlier in this book, lead to the habits which ultimately shape your reality. In light of this, I encourage you to be very mindful about the different environments and people you expose yourself to, as the path to achieving your dreams requires focus, stamina and strength. Exposing yourself to people and environments that empower and uplift you will help you to stay focused and maintain the right mindset for success. Being intentional about surrounding yourself around people who are moving in the same direction as you, and who have common interests to you, will offer you the support of a community which can be a powerful driving force. As humans we are social beings and although we can achieve great things on our own, we achieve so much more when we work together so finding the people who you can work well with is a worthwhile investment to make. You don't need to have several people walk your journey with you, but a few key individuals who you know support you and challenge you to be your best will go a long   way!

Chapter 8

Principle 4 – Mentorship and Collaboration

The journey towards your dream should not be in isolation.

Working towards a dream or accomplishing something great, is not a lone venture. When you make an effort to connect with individuals both within and outside of your network, you tap into a wealth of resources which can further accelerate your progress. Finding a mentor is a great place to start. A mentor is an individual who has already succeeded in an area you wish to succeed in, or who possesses a vast amount of knowledge in an area you are studying, and is able to guide you accordingly. They speak from a fountain of knowledge, expertise and wisdom, and they can help you avoid many of the mistakes they have made, and in doing so, fast track your progress. The relationship you have with a mentor could be very structured or it could be quite informal. A structured relationship might involve agreeing on specific meeting dates throughout the year where you touch base and assess your progression towards specific milestones you have already agreed on. A more informal relationship might involve freely being able to call your mentor when you have a question or need their advice. The type of mentor-mentee relationship you have will vary depending on your character and the character of your mentor. It is important that you respect the style your mentor prefers in order to maintain a good relationship with your mentor.

Along my journey, I have had several mentors who have supported me in different areas of my life. I think it is a good idea to have a range of mentors because different people will be skilled in different areas and ultimately, you want to seek the counsel of someone who is excelling in the specific area you wish to excel in. I have mentors that I seek advice for concerning my charity, concerning my leadership development, concerning my medical career, concerning my spiritual growth and concerning my fitness, to name a few. Having mentors to support me in each of these separate area helps me to grow and progress in all areas which is something I am committed to. I think it is very important to live a well-balanced life and so I try to develop all the areas that are important to me, rather than excelling in one area at the expense of the other.

People often ask me how to go about finding a mentor. The first piece of advice I would give, is have a clear understanding of your objective. If you have a clear objective and you share this with a prospective mentor, they are much more likely to be interested in supporting you as it gives them clarity over what they can offer. A mentor will want to feel like their involvement in your life is bearing some kind of fruit and so if you have a clear objective, this creates a measurable goal which offers a sense of achievement for both you and your mentor as you draw closer to, and eventually achieve that goal. The second piece of advice I would give is, where possible, try to focus on cultivating a relationship first before you ask for a person's guidance or mentorship. This may not always be achievable if the mentor you are seeking is not connected to your present social network. However, in situations where they are, it is a good idea to first focus on relationship building before you ask for their mentorship. Building a relationship first offers several advantages. It allows you to understand how your prospective mentor operates as an individual – what they like and dislike, their style of communication and leadership. Developing this understanding is useful because it will offer you insight into what working with this person could be like. If you notice that they're very structured in their approach to things, with little room for flexibility, and you're the opposite of this, you might decide that they're not the ideal mentor for you. Furthermore, understanding their style of working will help to cultivate the mentor-mentee relationship you eventually form. This is because you'll be able to adapt to their working style which will please them and therefore make for a more enjoyable and productive mentor-mentee relationship.

When you're seeking a mentor, think about what you might be able to offer to the relationship. Having a mindset of adding value, instead of only receiving value, can be a helpful approach to enjoying better relationships with people. This point may be harder to grapple with than the former points because often, when we think about a mentor, we automatically put the person on a pedestal as someone full of expertise who we are trying to glean from. However, the concept of reverse mentoring is something that is becoming much more recognised and celebrated. I have several mentors who are twice my age and have testified that through the mentor-mentee relationship we have, they have learnt a lot from me. One of my mentors who has played a significant role in a lot of my success to date, also calls me her mentor. To offer a practical example to help illustrate this point, if there is a prospective mentor you have who is working on a project, you could offer to support them in this project.

Since you'll be working with them on something that is important to them, they'll naturally be more inclined to offer their time to speak with you or meet up with you. Most of the focus of these meetings will likely be linked to the project, but as you're spending time around them, you'll be learning from them. In addition to this, you'll start developing a relationship with them so that in the future, if you have a specific request that you'd like from them, they'll be more inclined to say yes to you.

The person who you may be looking to as a potential mentor will probably have others who look to them in the same fashion. Some of the things that can help you stand out as someone worth their time include having an attitude of humility. Be willing to learn from what your mentor is sharing with you and even if something doesn't make sense to you, ask them for further clarity and be willing to try. If you agree to do something by a particular deadline, make sure you get it done. If things come up that may delay you in meeting that deadline, let them know in advance. These are simple points that are sometimes overlooked. It is important that you are very proactive as a mentee and when you can demonstrate an enthusiasm to learn and a commitment to implement what you're being taught, it demonstrates to your mentor that you are worth their investment in you.

For the second half of this chapter, I want to focus on the importance of collaborating with people. I mentioned at the very start that your journey towards your dream should not be a lone venture. You can achieve a lot by yourself, but the amount you can achieve when you start working with others become exponential. The reality is, you cannot be excellent in all areas and so collaborating with others helps to compensate for the areas where you're weak. The ability to recognise your weaknesses and begin working with people who are strong in those areas, will increase your chances of success and allow your ventures to excel at a much faster rate. Sometimes people are reluctant to collaborate with others because of their own insecurities. They feel intimidated about working with someone who is much better than they are in a certain area. However, this is not the right attitude to have. When you recognise the value that you can bring to the table, your fear of others shining more brightly than you starts to dissolve because you understand your lane of influence and you're focused on that. Furthermore, if the person or people you are working with are united by a common goal and focused on achieving this, you do not need to be intimidated by how skilled they are at a particular area because ultimately you are all on the same team!

The creation and development of my charity is a good example of collaboration. My charity began as a project which I started by myself. It was when I joined forces with my co-founder, Daniel Huf that things really started taking off. Daniel and I possess very different skills that work very well together. My business relationship with Daniel is probably one of the most synergistic relationships I have in my life. Firstly, he is not medical, he is more business and strategic-minded. He studied English literature at Cambridge and then went on to work as a strategy consultant for PwC, before moving on to study an MBA at Stanford, which is where he is now at the time of me writing this book. Daniel is extremely intelligent and articulate; he is a strategic thinker and is very logical in his approach to things. He works best under pressure, is very good at analysing the bigger picture and creating a strategy plan to reach this, and enjoys data and spreadsheets. In contrast, I am emotionally driven, I pay close attention to detail, I'm a socialite who is very good at creating and maintaining relationships, I extensively plan ahead so that I can avoid working under pressure, I am naturally a visionary and I do not enjoy analysing data or spreadsheets, though I recognise the importance of this! Despite our differences, Daniel and I are very similar in that we have a similar ethos, are driven by passion, we think on a global scale, we have an attitude of excellence and we are perfectionists. The beauty of our relationship is that in the areas where I am weak, Daniel tends to be strong and vice versa. Our different strengths and weaknesses also tend to balance each other out e.g., whereas I would arrive at a meeting one hour early, Daniel would arrive just on time and in some instances two to three minutes late. With us sometimes operating at either ends of an extreme, we tend to respectfully disagree with each other, which often helps us to find a middle ground, unless one of us is convinced that the other is completely bonkers.

Collaborating and working as part of a successful team requires more than just the technical skill you can contribute. There are several other interpersonal skills that you should work on developing in order to build and maintain good relationships. Investing your time in developing your communication skills, emotional intelligence and tolerance, for example, can be just as important as sharpening your technical skills. This is because working as part of a team means working effectively with people; your ability to do this will, to a large degree, depend on how well you can build and maintain relationships. If you spend enough time around someone, likelihood is you'll do something that will eventually irritate that person or cause offence. Being able to identify when you have caused offence, or being open to receiving feedback about an offence you've caused someone else, are very important skills to develop. Effective communication becomes paramount in these situations because the way you express yourself concerning sensitive issues can have the power to either diffuse a tense situation or make it ten times worse. Generally, people are quite forgiving if they feel they have been listened to and their frustrations acknowledged. However, sometimes we can be dismissive if we disagree with another person's point because it does not line up with our logic. This is where exercising empathy and humility become very important because whether the person expressing their concern is right or wrong, the fact of the matter is they feel offended. Being able to listen, to truly understand the person's perspective and the paradigm through which they're viewing the situation, will help you to at least understand why they feel offended, even if you do not agree with their logic. Demonstrating that you acknowledge and care for a person's feelings can go a long way. Saying, "I can hear how frustrated I have made you feel and I am sorry you feel that way. The reason I said what I said was because of…" is likely to fare much better than "I don't agree with what you're saying and I think you are being completely unreasonable. Look at this situation like this…" The second statement is likely to cause more offence than the first statement because it does not acknowledge the frustration or hurt the person feels, rather it completely dismisses both their feelings and their perspective. The first statement acknowledges how the person feels which is likely to make them more receptive to hearing your explanation and understanding your perspective. Investing in developing your communication skills and emotional intelligence is important because ultimately, we are all humans with emotions. In order to get the best out of someone, it is important that they feel valued, respected and appreciated. Your ability to respectfully reason with colleagues and acknowledge their feelings will help you to demonstrate your value and respect for them which is likely to strengthen and build relationships.

In my business relationship with Daniel, we have had several encounters where we've disagreed with each other or felt frustrated by how something has been handled. None of the issues have been major issues, however, left under the carpet, they would have impacted our business relationship. Being committed to open communication is one of the key things that has allowed us to overcome our disagreements and strengthen our relationship. Daniel and I truly care about how each other feel, we respect one another and we want to work well together. As such, we are open to rebuke and we walk in humility. If we are having a disagreement, we are not too prideful to acknowledge when we're in the wrong. Our disagreements have actually been a fundamental part of strengthening our relationship since it is through the disagreements that we have learnt more about each other and our working styles. The way that Daniel and I think about and prioritise tasks is different; in fact, the way our minds work is fundamentally different! Daniel is a strategic thinker and he has the natural tendency to focus on the bigger picture and the key strategic steps which will take us there. As a result of this, he is less likely to think about or focus on the smaller items on our priority list e.g., responding to an email. In our early stages when Daniel had this as a responsibility, I would sometimes become frustrated with him for not responding to emails as quickly as I would or forgetting to send them entirely. In those moments, I felt like he was being careless and not prioritising things that I considered to be important. However, through communicating with him, I realised that firstly he cared about how I felt and was not intentionally trying to stress me out and secondly, he genuinely tends to forget small tasks or places them on the bottom of his priority list which result in them being forgotten. As a result of this, we eventually concluded that it was better for me to focus on the relationship-management aspect of the charity and to have regular follow-ups with him as and when needed. In contrast, Daniel would focus more of his attention on our higher-level strategic priorities such as hiring staff and bid-writing. Naturally our responsibilities do overlap e.g., if I am arranging a meeting with a key contact, Daniel would come along to the meeting and similarly, if Daniel had shortlisted 7 candidates for a job role we advertised, together we would review the shortlisted CVs and carry out the interviews. However, by defining and agreeing on our key areas of focus, we have been able to function more effectively as co-founders which has translated into the continued growth and development of our charity.

When you can create an atmosphere of open communication where colleagues can feel comfortable to raise a concern and trust that their voice will be heard, it makes for a much healthier working environment. In addition to this, if you're in a leadership position, role modelling this becomes of utmost importance because ultimately, the ethos you create at the top of the organisation filters down. You have to live out the values that you want your organisation to encapsulate. Team-building activities can facilitate this process and they also help you to form personal connections with people outside of the work mode. Realistically, you will not become best buddies with all the people you work with. However, you can hold a mutual respect for each other and cultivating a working environment where the colleagues respect one another, will form a team that will work much more effectively. As a result of this, you'll be much more successful in carrying out the organisations mission and working towards the end goal.

Chapter 9

Principle 5 – Leading A Life of Discipline

Journeying towards your dream will require the disciplined version of you.

The online Cambridge dictionary defines self-discipline as "the ability to make yourself do things you know you should do even when you do not want to". Discipline is the art of being driven by purpose and principles, rather than emotions. Being driven by purpose means it's the end goal you have in mind which motivates you to remain committed. Being driven by principles means you make decisions based on what you believe to be right, even if this is inconvenient. When you're driven by purpose and principles, instead of your emotions, you'll find it becomes far easier to stick to your commitments. Exercising discipline on a consistent basis is not easy. It will require you to work through some uncomfortable feelings such as procrastination, apprehension, resistance and even pain. Although this process is challenging, you'll realise that the more you practise doing it, the easier it becomes. As your muscle of discipline is slowly strengthened, you begin to realise just how powerful your mind is. When you make up in your mind that you are going to be committed to something and give no room for excuses, you will be surprised by just how disciplined you can be. Leading a disciplined life is not something reserved for a special few. We all possess the power to be disciplined and it is something we must be intentional about. The process may not be linear, there will be moments when you may give in to temptation or succumb to procrastination. However, the more intentional you are about being disciplined, the more disciplined you will become.

The first step to leading a more disciplined life is finding a compelling reason. If you lack mental clarity over the benefits of being disciplined, you will struggle. This is because when your emotions are raging against you, it is reminding yourself of the overall purpose that will empower you to keep going. There are a number of generic reasons as to why we should lead a disciplined lifestyle, however, the more you can personalise the reason, the easier it becomes. For example, imagine your doctor were to tell you that you are pre-diabetic and unless you change your lifestyle, you are at great risk of becoming diabetic. Trying to prevent yourself from becoming diabetic could be a powerful driving force helping you to lead a disciplined life in the area of health and fitness. You could strengthen your commitment to this by doing some research into the health complications associated with diabetes and how these could stop you from leading the life of freedom that you once enjoyed. Being motivated by a desire to be healthy and to enjoy the benefits that come with this, could offer you a very powerful reason to commit to a life of discipline in relation to your health.

As human beings, we are emotional creatures. Sometimes we can start the day feeling super motivated and inspired to crush our goals, but by the afternoon, perhaps something unexpected happens or we have a disagreement with someone that triggers negative emotions within us. With the surfacing of these negative emotions, the initial motivation and zeal we started the day with begins to subside and as such, our desire to commit to the plans we had for that day may begin to wane. This is when discipline becomes key since it's your commitment to your overall vision and goal that will empower you to continue with the tasks you set out to do, despite the lack of enthusiasm you feel. Being able to exercise this kind of discipline on a day-to-day basis is of paramount importance, particularly when you find yourself in leadership positions bearing great responsibility. Emotions can be very unstable and unreliable as depending on the day's events, you could experience great joy and great excitement as well as great anger and great frustration. If you are led by your emotions, you will find it very difficult to see the results you want in the time frames you set as your emotions will frequently lead you off track. The other important thing to remember is that emotions often follow action! When you decide to push past the initial procrastination and get started on a task, you begin to find yourself become more engaged and motivated to continue. For me, a classic example of this is going to the gym. Despite my love for fitness, sometimes I do not feel like exercising. However, once I get started, I find myself becoming more motivated to continue. Being able to master and discipline your emotions so that they are not able to dictate your actions is a great skill to develop. I also want to remind you that becoming a more disciplined person is not something that will happen instantaneously, it is a journey and a non-linear one at that. You may have days when you feel like you've been exceptionally disciplined, and equally, you may have days where you feel like you've lifted all your boundaries and have been the most ill-disciplined person on earth. The key thing here, is to remember that every day is a new day. Every decision you make matters and you possess the power to turn a new leaf, and start again. What matters is that overall, you are moving in the direction of a more disciplined life.

In some instances, you do need to listen to your emotions first. For example, if you are starting to feel burnt out and as a result, you're experiencing the emotion of exhaustion, it is important that you listen to your body and take adequate rest. Finding a balance between resting and executing your vision is very important because ultimately, you want to find a routine that is sustainable so that you can steadily work towards achieving your goals over a prolonged period of time. If you're trying to sprint a marathon, you will not reach the finish line because you'll expend all of your energy in the first few miles of the race. In the same manner, the journey towards your dream is a journey which will require you to pace yourself. Being able to listen to your body and discern procrastination versus genuine fatigue is an important skill. There are some clear signs that will help you to differentiate between the two. When you are nearing burn out you may feel exhausted all the time, struggle to concentrate, struggle to be motivated, you may feel overwhelmed; and you may feel disillusioned about your vision all together. If you suspect you're leaning towards burn out be sure to take a step back, to revaluate your current commitments and to slow down. I also want to encourage you not to be afraid to relinquish certain responsibilities if you need to. Sometimes, particularly when you're a very ambitious person who pushes themselves, there can be a sense of failure that you feel at the thought of relinquishing a responsibility you've committed to. However, this should not be the case. Your ability to recognise that you're struggling to juggle all the balls placed in your hands and to let some go, is just as much of a great skill as commitment is. In fact, the ability to do this demonstrates both wisdom and commitment. The more you juggle, the less time and effort you will have to commit to each responsibility. As such, being able to let some things go, frees up more of your time to focus on the few things you've prioritised which allows you to be even more committed to what is important. The final point I want to make on this matter is not allowing yourself to be guilt-tripped into holding on to a responsibility that is weighing you down. We live in a society where most people care about their own priorities above yours. Sometimes, another person is so fixated on achieving their goal that they want your support in making it happen, even if you express that you're struggling to cope. This is where you need to exercise a level of "selfishness" by prioritising your own well-being. After all, if you are burnt out and struggling to cope, you are not going to be useful to anyone and so it is important that you prioritise your well-being above all.

Now that I've highlighted why leading a disciplined lifestyle is so important, I want to explore some of the practical tools you can implement to help you become a more disciplined person. Firstly, I want to touch on your mindset because discipline starts in the mind. You have to decide in your mind that you want to lead a disciplined lifestyle because your thoughts influence your actions. Listening to podcasts or some kind of inspirational message to reinforce to you the importance of leading a disciplined lifestyle can help you focus on the thoughts that are in alignment with a disciplined lifestyle. Doing this as part of your daily practice or several times throughout the week will help to keep you motivated. As well as being disciplined in your actions, it is important that you are disciplined in your mind. We all have negative thoughts that may enter our mind and question our ability to achieve our goals. When you focus on and feed these thoughts, they start to magnify and the consequence of this is reduced self-esteem. However, learning to silence these thoughts and choosing to believe in your potential to achieve your dreams, will help you to continue driving forwards towards your goals. The messages that you repeatedly listen to and the environments that you consistently expose yourself to, will all shape your mindset. This is why it is important to separate yourself from toxic people, toxic messages and toxic environments where it is within your power to do so. We live in a world that is full of so much negativity and so many dream killers. As such, it is important that you consciously make the effort to surround yourself with the people and the things that empower you to believe in your potential and challenge you to manifest your potential.

Your desire to attain your goal needs to supersede your desire to do otherwise. For example, if you want to lose weight, your desire to lose weight needs to outweigh your desire to be stagnant and eat whatever you feel like whenever you feel like. Temptation to give in to unhealthy habits or the thing that is drawing you away from your goal, becomes weaker when you focus your attention on the benefits of attaining your goal. As such, if you can spend time really nailing down why you want to achieve the particular goal you have it can help to increase the intensity of your desire. Asking, and answering, certain questions related to your goal can help you magnify your desire for the goal. For example, if you were overweight and you decided you wanted to lose 10kg to become a healthier weight, you could ask yourself the following questions:

- What would being 10kg less feel like?

- What would being 10kg less look like?

- How would being 10kg less influence my perception about myself?

- How would being 10kg less influence other people's perception of me?

- How would being 10kg less influence my health?

- How would being 10kg less influence my mental health?

By answering these questions, you're giving yourself much more clarity over the benefits associated with achieving your goal. This clarity can serve as a powerful driving force which empowers you to say no to temptation because you're no longer motivated by instant gratification, but rather, by the benefits attached to reaching your future goal. Going through this process once is not enough as it is very easy to forget the benefits of working diligently towards your goal. In order to keep these benefits at the forefront of your mind, it would be a good idea to have them written down somewhere where you can daily review them, particularly at the beginning of your day before you are been confronted with the temptation that may meet you during the day.

The 1% effect is a mindset that I love to use to help me as I journey towards my own goals. It's based on the principle that a little effort, applied consistently over a prolonged period of time compounds. Since only a little effort is needed, it helps you overcome the procrastination linked to approaching a seemingly overwhelming task by setting the bar very low for what you need to achieve. For example, if you set yourself the goal to write a book, the thought of writing an entire book can seem very overwhelming and daunting. There are several steps involved in writing a book including planning the content, writing the content, designing the book cover, organising the publishing, organising the printing, and marketing the book. Breaking these steps into bite-sized chunks can help, but this can still feel a little daunting. As such, you may have an increased tendency to procrastinate or avoid writing your book. Based on the 1% effect, you might set yourself a small goal of writing two sentences of the book per day. You are more likely to perceive this goal as achievable because compared to writing 30-40 000 words, it seems like a small amount of effort. As a result of this, you'll find it much easier to be consistent with writing two sentences per day, which will compound and result in a book over time. The other benefit of this mindset is that, once you start writing the two sentences, you are likely to feel motivated to write more, which is a bonus. However, because the daily goal is only to write two sentences, so long as you meet this target there is no sense of shame associated with failing to meet your daily goal. People often underestimate the power of consistent effort applied over a long period of time. On the journey towards achieving your goal, prioritise consistency over productivity. There are some days when you may feel like you are much less productive than other days, but developing a habit of consistency means that so long as you keep working towards your goal, overall, you're likely to have more productive days than non-productive days and these compound!

As you commit to leading a life of discipline, one of the things you'll need to be mindful of is the all-or-nothing mentality. This is not an issue for everyone, but for some of us it can be a great hindrance to our progression. The all-or-nothing mentality results in you focusing on either extreme of a spectrum rather than finding a balanced medium, which overall, will help you to journey towards your goal at a faster pace. The all-or-nothing mentality says that if I have eaten a spoonful of the cake, when I made the commitment to abstain from cake, since I've already had a spoonful, I might as well eat the entire cake. The all-or-nothing mentality says that I wasn't going to watch Netflix this week, but since I have already watched one show on the second day of this week, I might as well continue watching shows for the remainder of this week and start again next week. This is a very black-and-white mindset which is not best suited to an extremely colourful world. You have to accept that as a human you are inherently imperfect, sometimes we will not perform our best and we may falter in areas we were committed to being strong. Being able to forgive yourself for these moments of faltering and to encourage yourself to keep persevering should be your focus. This is not the easiest thing to do, particularly if you are someone who naturally has an extreme personality, like myself for example. I particularly struggled with an all-or-nothing mentality in my fitness journey. I would become so frustrated and angry with myself for not sticking to the regimented fitness and food plans I would create for myself and if I faltered, I would often allow myself to fall totally off the bandwagon. However, being able to recognise this pattern and challenge it is what helped me to change it. The process of changing it involved extending a portion of grace to myself. It involved me celebrating myself for how much effort I had put in and reassuring myself that a few slip ups are minor in comparison to the grand scheme of things and that my overall performance is shaped by my overall consistency. Sometimes we can condemn and rebuke ourselves far more harshly than we would ever do to someone else. Being able to cut yourself some slack and encourage yourself to try again is an important aspect of overcoming the all-or-nothing mentality and persevering towards your goals. In addition to this, sometimes if you find that you're continually slipping up or not meeting a goal you have set yourself, it could be an indication that you need to revaluate your goal. It might not be the case that your goal is unattainable, it might just mean you need to give yourself a little bit more flexibility on the journey towards meeting it. For example, if your goal is to exercise five times per week but you're struggling to commit to this. Adjusting this goal to three exercise sessions per week and being more mindful of your diet might be a more effective strategy for you. Being able to reflect on your progress towards a goal, and adjust your strategy accordingly, will go a long way in helping you to remain consistent in leading a more disciplined life.

Chapter 10

Principle 6 – Facing Fear

The journey towards your dream will require you to stand up in the face of fear.

The Cambridge online dictionary defines fear as "an unpleasant emotion or thought that you have when you are frightened or worried by something dangerous, painful or bad that is happening or might happen". Fear is an emotion that all human beings can relate to and most of us would agree that it is mostly an unpleasant feeling. There are different types of fear and different intensities of the emotion. The fear you might feel because you are about to give an important speech versus the fear you would feel if someone was pointing a gun at your head and threatening to kill you, are two very different types of fear which would involve very different emotional and physical responses. Weirdly, sometimes people find fear pleasurable... This is the reason why people will watch a horror movie – the anticipation of fear causes a sense of excitement. However, fear-inspired excitement is mostly a result of anticipated fear which you can, to some degree, control. A person going to watch a horror movie predicts that they're going to experience the emotion of fear and this creates a sense of excitement. In contrast, when we cannot anticipate the outcome of a situation or circumstance that concerns us, this usually does not excite us! Fear is a spectrum and it is a very subjective emotion as two people could encounter the same "frightening" stimulus and respond completely different.

In this chapter, I want to focus on the fear that threatens to stop you from achieving your dreams. It is the fear that tells you that you're not equipped, that you're not talented enough and that if you go ahead with this venture or opportunity, you're going to make a fool of yourself. It is the fear that makes you worry about the future e.g., "if I decide to quit my job and pursue my dream, will I be able to afford to live, what will people think of me if I fail, what will I think of myself?" It is not wrong to feel the emotion of fear and to ponder these fear-provoking questions in your mind. However, the issue arises when you're making decisions and choices led by fear. This is because fear is something that will always be there, it is an emotion that is part of the human experience. Trying to mitigate the emotion by living a life that is below what you know you're capable of, is not the solution that will allow you to achieve your dreams. On the journey towards manifesting your vision you have to choose to be bold, you have to choose to stand up to fear because you believe that you have what it takes to achieve your dream and you're willing to fight for this. Oftentimes, when we challenge our fears, we realise that the situation is never as bad as we thought it would be! Even in circumstances where what we feared does happen, so long as you're alive, there is still the opportunity to grow, to develop, to learn, and to move forwards. Most of what I have achieved to date, and many of the upcoming opportunities I have, have triggered an emotion of fear within me. Over time by repeatedly challenging this emotion, I have become more comfortable with feeling fear and acting anyway; as the famous phrase goes "feel the fear and do it anyway!" I want to encourage you that feeling fear doesn't make you less than, it doesn't suggest that you don't possess what it takes to succeed! In contrast, it reminds you that you're human, it reminds you that you care so much about the venture you're about to take on that you don't want to mess it up. It allows you to empathise and relate to other people and it reminds you of just how strong you are, that you would feel an emotion that could paralyse your dream but instead, you choose to take action!

Choosing to stand up to fear can be a very daunting experience. It often overwhelms your senses and makes it difficult to think straight. However, you have the power to stand up against it, and you have to believe this. Before you conquer physically, you have to conquer mentally because it is your mindset that will determine your actions which will either move you closer towards, or further from, your dream. If you speak to an athlete, they'll often say that before they physically cross the finish line, they envision themselves crossing it in their mind. Your mind is the most powerful tool you have in this life and it is important to learn how to use it to your advantage. Focusing your mind on thoughts that will empower you and fill you with courage, is the thing to do when facing a challenge that naturally causes you to feel fearful. Your initial tendency when faced with a situation like this is to question your ability, doubt your potential, and subsequently; begin to feel insecure, timid and incapable. However, if you choose to refocus your mind on thoughts that will empower you, you can disrupt this process and as a result, you will begin to feel a greater sense of confidence and capability. Focusing on the power of your *why* is a key tool to help create this mental shift. By focusing on your *why*, you are reminding yourself of your overall goal and this will inspire you to challenge fear in order to move closer towards your vision. It is important to remember that whatever you focus on grows and whatever you starve dies. If you're preoccupying your mind with thoughts that are provoking more fear in you, or listening to people who are reinforcing the fear, this is not going to fill you with the courage needed to challenge fear. Rather, you are going to magnify fear in your mind which will make you feel almost powerless to confront the situation that lies ahead. However, when you begin to shift your focus from the fear onto what life on the other side of fear could look like, this begins to empower you. Most people will testify that the things they were scared of were often never as bad as they thought they would be. We can take comfort from this because it reassures us that usually, the intensity of the negative anticipation we have is unwarranted. When your desire and hunger for achieving your dream becomes stronger than the fear inspired by thoughts of what could go wrong, you'll find it much easier to stand up in the face of fear. The truth of the matter is, you cannot guarantee that if you challenge fear and do the thing you're scared of, it will all work out just as you have hoped. However, if you choose to be subdued by fear and not to pursue your dreams, you can guarantee that you will not achieve them. Becoming fearless doesn't mean that you do not feel fear, it means that you do not allow fear to control your actions. When you allow your actions to be controlled by your principles and the overall vision you have for your life, you'll find that your path towards your dream becomes clearer.

Another practical measure you can take to help you stand up against fear, is interpreting the emotion as excitement. Fear and excitement actually produce a very similar physiological response – meaning your body responds to these different emotions in a similar way. Fear and excitement both stimulate your sympathetic nervous system, commonly referred to as the fight, flight or freeze response. This commonly causes your heart rate and breathing rate to increase, your palms become sweaty, you feel a butterfly sensation in your stomach and mentally, you tend to feel more alert and a little on edge. When you can interpret these feelings as excitement, rather than fear, it helps you to think from a more positive perspective and rather than wanting to run away from the situation, you will feel more empowered to face the challenge head-on. The more you challenge fear and experience this physiological response, the more familiar the feelings become. The familiarity doesn't take away the sense of fear, but it does help you to get a better handle on your emotions and your body's physiological response. To give you an example, when I first started my journey of public speaking, as mentioned earlier in this book, I used to be terrified. The physiological response stimulated when I gave my first speech in front of a large crowd was very difficult to control. My heart thumped in my chest, my voice quavered and my hands shook violently. I found this experience deeply humiliating! In spite of this, deep down there was something inside of me that was convinced that public speaking was an area of life I was called to master in. I knew that the only way to improve would be to keep exposing myself to these types of situations so that I could get more practise. Even though this sometimes felt like self-inflicted trauma, I was convinced that the more I did it, the better I would become. My conviction was correct. The more I spoke on various stages to various crowds, the more confident I became. Studies have also demonstrated that repeated exposure to the same stressor reduces the intensity of your emotional response. The first exposure might cause a feeling of intense and overwhelming fear, but over time, the intensity of this emotional response begins to wane. Based on this fact, as well as physically exposing yourself to the stressor, you can mentally expose yourself to it which also can help to calm your nerves down when faced with the real situation. To use an example, before any important speech I have, I always envision myself on the stage. I envision myself standing behind the podium in front of the crowd with the light, and people's gaze centred on me. By doing this, I'm mentally preparing myself for the speech by recreating a situation, in my mind, which makes me feel nervous. This helps me to feel more relaxed on the day of my speech as the situation doesn't feel so novel. Up until now I still feel nervous before a speech, however, I am able to control my emotions much more effectively than I was able to in my early stages of public speaking. I actively calm myself down by positive talk minutes before a speech and though I feel a sense of anxiety, I interpret this as excitement. Usually, after about a minute of speaking I am into the flow of things and I can continue without being overwhelmed by my body's physiological response to the situation.

If interpreting the sensation of fear as excitement does not help you, just accept the emotion for what it is. Have the mindset that you are going to feel the unpleasant emotion of fear and your body may respond to it, but irrespective, you are determined to carry out the task you've set forth to do. Focus on your *why* and have your vision at the forefront of your mind and this will empower you to face the fear because you've given purpose to it. It is important to stand up to fear and walk in courage because by doing this, you're developing a habit of being led by your vision and not by your emotions. If you surrender to fear, it becomes even harder to stand up against it the next time you're challenged by it.

Rewarding yourself for challenging fear is another driving force that can help you to overcome it. By offering yourself an immediate reward, you can focus on the pleasure of attaining that reward which you know is literally on the other side of you challenging the fearful situation. This can sometimes be more helpful than focusing on your vision because your vision is usually a long-term goal you're working towards. As such, you may struggle to see the immediate benefit of how challenging fear translates to the manifestation of your overall vision. Celebrating yourself for challenging fear is really important because it takes a lot of courage to persevere through the unpleasant emotions and the physiological response that comes with persevering at something that scares you. By celebrating yourself, you are reinforcing the importance of challenging fear and you're beginning to associate positivity with an experience that inherently feels negative. As a result, the paradigm through which you interpret fear starts to shift from an uncomfortable and negative experience to an opportunity to exercise character strength and be rewarded for doing so.

Asking yourself, "What is the worse that could happen to me?" is another strategy you can use to help you challenge fear. When I'm feeling particularly scared about an opportunity I know is great for me, I ask myself this question. I reason in my mind that the worst possible outcome is death. Most of the situations we fear will not result in death and so I encourage myself from thereon, that anything else that happens will be survivable. If we are honest with ourselves, fear is often rooted in pride. We worry about how others will perceive us if we fail or don't perform to a certain standard. Being able to challenge your pride is important because if we are controlled by pride, we are going to restrict what is possible for us as our actions will be controlled by fear of other people's perceptions instead of the vision we have for our future. Part of the process of overcoming fear requires us to make up in our mind that other people's opinions and perceptions of us is not as important as our perception of ourselves. Your ability to stand up in the face of fear has a lot to do with your perception about yourself. If you see yourself as someone who is capable of succeeding, you will find it easier to stand up to fear even at the possibility of you making a mess of the situation. It is important to be gracious towards yourself and remind yourself that you're on a journey of self-development. Even if you do not perform how you hoped, the mere fact that you were bold enough to take a step that would help draw you closer to your dreams is a win within itself. The more you actively engage in opportunities which challenge and stretch you, the more you'll grow and become better at your craft. You have to remind yourself that the people we look to and admire as giants in their field, are often closer to a finished product. When they started out, they were not as excellent and brilliant as they are today. They always had the potential to be excellent, but they underwent a process of refining which allowed their excellence to be reflected on the outside. We live in a microwave generation that is fixated on doing everything as quickly and as conveniently as possible. The danger with this is that, sometimes we get frustrated by our speed of progress for processes which inherently take time. The development of your character is not something that happens overnight. Becoming the version of yourself that you envision is, in most cases, a journey which requires consistency, commitment and perseverance. Being able to challenge fear is a part of this process and you have to accept that increased boldness, tenacity and self-confidence come with time.

Ultimately, the reality is that the journey towards pursuing your dream is not going to be a walk in the park. Fear, amongst other challenges, will serve to potentially side track, stop, or pull you away from your dream. You have to make the decision that you are either going to allow this to happen, or you are going to challenge fear. You have to decide whether you want to stay in the safety of your comfort zone, or push past it into the realm of uncertainty which also becomes the realm of unlimited potential. Restricting yourself to the zone of comfortability, the zone of predictability and the zone of safety, will not challenge you to change. Life is a journey that is supposed to involve the evolution of your character and the unravelling of your potential. This can only be achieved when you choose to step out of your normal routine and do something different. You realise that when you begin to do this, not only do you start to lead a more interesting and exciting life, you'll be better positioned to positively influence and impact those around you.

Chapter 11

Principle 7 – Healing from Pain

The journey towards you dream becomes easier when you choose to let go of the hurt and pain that is weighing you down.

Emotional hurt is not the most exciting topic to talk about. When we think about implementing strategies to achieve a goal, we don't often think about a strategy linked to our emotional healing. However, I would argue that this is just as important as any of the strategies we've already discussed, and potentially, even of greatest importance. As humans we are emotional creatures, how we feel directly impacts our focus, our energy levels, and therefore our productivity. As such, being attentive to your overall emotional state and working on resolving some of the inner issues that weigh down your soul are important. Emotional healing is a process that can last an entire lifetime. That may sound a little daunting at first, but as we journey through life new experiences may potentially act as triggers which take us back to challenging places and induce a negative emotional response. Being able to work through this in a healthy manner is important. As we work through these issues, we become stronger and more resilient over time. If you dig deep enough, you'll often notice that the bad habits people engage in, whether that be comfort eating, smoking excessively or sleeping around; are often rooted in pain they're experiencing because of trauma they've hidden under the carpet. Being able to adopt a position of vulnerability by opening up your heart and being honest with yourself about the things that hurt you, is the first step to receiving emotional healing. It is not an easy thing to do and you have to decide whether it is something you want to do and if so, when is an appropriate time for you to invest in your emotional healing. However, I can certainty testify that it is one of the best investments one could ever make. When you become more whole in the area of your emotions, you become so much more stable, reliable and consistent as a person. You're able to handle the stresses and strains of life in a more balanced and rational way. You are less likely to make decisions based on impulse and intense emotions and you're more likely to judge from a place of reason and perspective. Emotional healing offers you a greater sense of emotional stability which helps you to better relate to yourself and those around you.

In my life, there have been two key emotional challenges that I have had to work on in order to excel in my purpose. The first emotional challenge was meeting my father for the first time when I was 19 years old. I had many questions and on a subconscious level, I was hurting in ways that were not always obvious to me. In addition, trying to build such an intimate relationship at a time in my life when I was discovering and forming my identity as a woman, was not easy. I remember the first time my father and I went out together, I was so surprised by human genetics! As I asked my father questions and he answered them, I was able to see the unravelling of his character which amazed me because I realised that I was so much like him. My father shared his stories with me about the poverty he overcame in Sierra Leone, he spoke about how he travelled to the UK and managed to secure a place at university to study nursing. He spoke about being so hungry one day and only having £10 to spare. He used his £10 in a Chinese restaurant and waited with great anticipation for the food. When he saw the size of the portion on his plate, his heart sank because it was not sufficient to satisfy his hunger and that was all the money he had. As my father shared his stories and I learnt about the great hardships he had overcome, I was filled with inspiration. I was able to see the tenacious and ferocious drive I have, in my father. It felt quite amazing to me to know that I was so much like someone who I knew so little about.

My father is a serious but laid-back character, he has a sense of humour and is very strong-willed. He has a caring nature and feels a sense of pride in being able to support and help those around him. He is a hard worker and is driven by his goals and dreams for the future. My father has a very stubborn nature and I too, can be quite stubborn sometimes. This is probably what has made our relationship quite challenging at times, particularly when we view situations from different paradigms. One of the greatest challenges we've had in our relationship thus far, is linked to our cultural differences. In many African cultures, it is the responsibility of the child to reach out to the parents. As such, if the child doesn't call their mother or father, they shouldn't expect to speak anytime soon. At face value, this may sound small but it is something I greatly struggled with. I found it difficult feeling like I was pursuing a father who had been absent for most of my life. His actions didn't make sense to me. I would explain this to him and although he would empathise with me, it was almost like he was wired this way and so the challenge would repeat itself. This would make me feel really hurt and quite resentful towards him, particularly because people would always tell me that your parents must be so proud of you and they must love having such an amazing daughter like you. Hearing this but feeling like my father was not making a consistent effort to develop our relationship was not easy for me. It felt like we had a yo-yo relationship in that there would be seasons of good communication intermingled with periods of silence. I am someone who is big on communication, being able to express my feelings and knowing that they've been heard is very important to me in relationships. As a result, the inconsistency in communication was impacting me emotionally. After thinking and praying, I decided that it would be healthier for me to step back altogether. I made this decision because I wanted to protect my own emotional wellbeing by preventing myself from being actively involved in what felt like an unstable relationship that was having a negative impact on my emotions. Sometimes in life, we have to choose to make decisions that might seem controversial, wrong, and disrespectful to some; but they're right for you. Ultimately, you have to deal with the emotional consequences of your actions and I knew that at a very high-pressured season in my life, when I was balancing my medical degree alongside the formation of my charity and speaking engagements, having additional emotional stressors that I could eliminate was not helpful. As such, I decided to eliminate the ones I had the power over and that included taking a break from the relationship with my father. During this time, I prayed a lot about the situation and focused on myself. I also engaged in therapy for a period of time which I found to be very helpful and would definitely encourage others to consider it as an option. Therapy is not so much of a taboo topic as it was in the past, however, I still think there is some hesitancy that people experience when they consider it as an option. Therapy in essence, is a safe place to speak. It's an environment where you can express your emotions without fear of judgement. You may not even understand your emotions, let alone how to express them, and that's okay. Just being free to say whatever comes up for you, and having someone validate that it is okay for you to experience those emotions can be very powerful. In addition to this, therapy can often be a good tool to help you better understand your own opinion on matters as it helps to draw out how you truly feel and think about something which might have been drowned in other people's opinions. Through therapy and prayer, I was able to come to a place of peace concerning the relationship between my father and me.

The other emotional challenge I had to work on took place in my early twenties. I was twenty-one years old and I thought I had met the man I would marry; I was utterly convinced of this in fact. He seemed to be everything I hoped for in a husband – we shared the same faith, he was driven and ambitious, he enjoyed working out at the gym, he was confident, charismatic, fun to be around, a non-conformist, tall, and I felt very strongly connected to him. I had never felt such a deep love for a man like this before and he seemed like my dream guy. When I shared this with my sister, who is one of the closest people to me, she too was convinced I had met my husband. When I discussed it with another friend whose perspective I deeply respect, she also thought this could be my husband. However, my friendship with this man became very challenging for me because he wasn't committing to anything and as time went on, I found this more and more difficult. Since we were both Christians who were active in our faith, I asked him to pray to God to receive clarity so that I could know where I stand. I had an upcoming trip to the Philippines during which I would be away for 28 days and he agreed that during this time he would pray and fast to receive clarity. During those 28 days he did not communicate with me at all. On my return from the Philippines, I reached out to him and I asked if he had received any clarity and he told me he did. He said to me that, "God said you're not my wife" and then proceeded to explain that he did not receive clarity about whether this meant I was not his wife now or not his wife at all, meaning there was a possibility that I could be his wife in the future. As a young lady who felt totally in love, I held onto the hope that maybe there could still be a future. However, as the months passed, the lack of commitment about the future left me in a limbo land which was making me feel really low. I asked him for complete clarity because of the emotional turmoil I was feeling and eventually he told me that I definitely was not his wife and there was no future possibility of this. When I heard this, I felt utterly heartbroken. I told him that I couldn't stay in contact with him and ended our friendship. This was the first time in my life I had experienced heart break and I struggled with it in ways it's hard to describe. I felt like my dream for the future had been crushed, I felt hopeless and confused. What made this experience exceptionally difficult for me, is that since becoming a Christian at the age of 15, my faith has always been the solid ground that has kept me sturdy. However, because I had put the man I thought I would marry on a spiritual pedestal, I naïvely believed his words. I genuinely believed that God told him he could not marry me and that this was not his choice. Once when we were in his car, he even said to me, "I would marry you next week but God said no". I was totally convinced that God was the entity prohibiting our potential union and not necessarily him. Looking back, this sounds ridiculous to me and I know that it was his decision for whatever reason. However, as a naïve 21-year-old, I believed him and because of this, I felt rejected by a God who I thought loved me and wanted the best for me. I felt as though I was not good enough and I struggled to recognise the God I previously depended on for everything. Experiencing this crisis in my faith alongside a broken heart and a low mood was not a fun experience. At the time, I had taken a year out of medical school to study an intercalated BSc degree in Global Health at King's College London. This is a 3-year degree condensed into a year so it was a very academically intense course. Trying to stay focused when my mind felt all over the place and my heart was aching so terribly, was extremely challenging for me. I would read through papers and I couldn't retain anything. I would cry in between revision. I struggled to concentrate in lectures and I was completely convinced at one point that I was going to fail the course. I remember encouraging myself in my bedroom that even if I failed, this was an additional degree so it wouldn't matter as much. Thankfully, by the grace of God I pulled through and managed to secure a 2:1.

As time persisted, the emotional intensity of the heartache began to wane and slowly, I started becoming enlightened by the truth that I had indeed placed this man on a pedestal and he was not who I made him out to be in my mind. What helped me during this time was speaking with people I trusted, counselling, and rebuilding my relationship with God. It felt like a very long process and it was probably one of the most difficult times of my life, however, as time passed, I felt stronger and my heart began to heal. There were definitely moments when I felt extremely resentful towards the guy, especially when I realised how naïve I had been to believe what he told me. However, being able to forgive people is of immense importance when it comes to maintaining a healthy soul. When you carry resentment, bitterness and unforgiveness in your heart, these things weigh you down. There is a famous saying which I feel powerfully encapsulates why we should choose to forgive. The saying is "unforgiveness is like drinking poison yourself and waiting for the other person to die" and in essence, it is making the point that the pain you feel from choosing to hate and hold resentment to another person is actually causing you deep pain and emotional trauma. Choosing to forgive the person who has caused you great offence is not for them, really it is for you! When you can free your heart of toxic emotions, you feel lighter, your mood improves and your mind has better clarity to focus on what is truly important. Choosing to forgive my father and choosing to forgive the man who I thought I would marry were two very important steps in my journey of self-healing. What helped me to forgive them was acknowledging that deep down they meant well. I know my father loves me in his own way and I know the man I thought I would marry did not intend to hurt me in the way he did. However, the reality is as long as we are humans who interact with other humans, we will encounter hurt. Choosing to move on from hurt is not easy but it is within your power to do so. You can make the decision that you no longer wish to be bound by depression and anger caused by harbouring bitterness and unforgiveness in your heart. You can choose to release the pain and choose to love. Choosing to love does not mean you need to be friends with the people who have hurt you, choosing to love means that you release them from your heart, you hold no animosity and you wish no evil towards them. It is probably one of the hardest things to do, but equally it is one of the most freeing experiences you could ever have.

It is my hope that through my transparency and vulnerability, you can find the courage to look inside of yourself and identify the parts of you that are deeply hurting. After identifying and coming to terms with this, I encourage you to seek support in order to go on your own journey of self-healing. This could be in the form of counselling or therapy, it could be in the form of prayer if you have a faith, or it could be talking with friends and loved ones. It is important that if you disclose matters of your heart with someone, it is with someone you know you can trust and who will keep your business confidential. I also want to encourage you that the journey of self-healing is not linear. You may have ups and downs, you may feel strong some days and weaker on other days, but overall, you will be moving in a forward direction. As I said at the beginning of the chapter, your overall emotional state has a huge bearing on your productivity and overall success. Investing in your emotional well-being is just as important as investing in your intellectual and material wellbeing. You don't have to start your emotional healing journey immediately, but please do not eliminate it from your thoughts when you reflect and plan your journey towards your own dreams.

Final Words

Thank you for taking the time to read my book. I hope that through sharing my story with you, you've been inspired and encouraged to keep persevering towards your goals and your dreams for the future. I hope that the seven principles with practical strategies I've offered you, are ones that you can implement in your own life. I'm confident that in doing so, you'll journey closer towards the life you envision for yourself. You are the master of your destiny and no matter what your starting point is, or how low you may feel you've fallen; you can choose to pick yourself back up. You can choose to start again and to believe again. I wish you every success along your journey towards pursuing your dream and I encourage you to lend a helping hand to those coming up behind you, where it's within your power to do so.

Printed in Great Britain
by Amazon

78456334R00072